CRYSTAL PALACE
On This Day

CRYSTAL PALACE
On This Day

*History, Facts & Figures
from Every Day of the Year*

NEIL McSTEEN

CRYSTAL PALACE
On This Day
History, Facts & Figures from Every Day of the Year

All statistics, facts and figures are correct as of 1st September 2008

© Neil McSteen

Neil McSteen has asserted his rights in accordance with the Copyright, Designs and Patents Act 1988 to be identified as the author of this work.

Published By:
Pitch Publishing (Brighton) Ltd
A2 Yeoman Gate
Yeoman Way
Durrington
BN13 3QZ

Email: info@pitchpublishing.co.uk
Web: www.pitchpublishing.co.uk

First published 2008

All rights reserved. No part of this publication may be reproduced, stored in a retrieval system, or transmitted in any form or by any means, electronic, mechanical, photocopying, recording or otherwise, without the prior permission in writing of the publisher and the copyright owners.

A catalogue record for this book is available from the British Library.

10-digit ISBN: 1-9054112-6-X
13-digit ISBN: 978-1-9054112-6-9

Typesetting and origination by Pitch Publishing
Printed in Great Britain by CPI Group (UK) Ltd, Croydon CR0 4YY

This book is dedicated to my immediate Crystal Palace family: Andrew McSteen, Ken McSteen, Ann McSteen, William McSteen, Linda Debrah-McSteen AND Hugh Todd.

Neil McSteen – September 2008

ACKNOWLEDGEMENTS

Many thanks must go to Dan Tester at Pitch Publishing for allowing me to write this book and for putting him through numerous entries about Br*g*t*n getting beaten at Selhurst Park. Again.

A massive thank you must also go to the Reverend Nigel Sands and Ian King. The Reverend's books on Palace have been invaluable, especially *The Men Who Made Crystal Palace Football Club*, *Crystal Palace FC: The A-Z*, *100 Years of Crystal Palace Football Club* and *Crystal Palace Football Club 1905-1995*. Similarly, Ian King's historical programme notes through the years have been the source of many gems of information. I must also thank Ian for his personal help on a few tricky dates.

Don Madgwick's *Palace Heroes & Legends*, Roy Peskett's *The Crystal Palace Story*, Dominic and Andrew Fifield's *Crystal Palace FC Centenary Book* were also extremely useful, as was the seminal We All Follow The Palace from Eagle Eye Publications. John Williams from Channel 4 and the Scottish FA also deserve thanks.

Last, and by no means least, I would like to extend my unswerving gratitude to the following characters who have all helped me in their own way with this book; Terry Byfield, Quayne Birch, Dan Botten, Richard Cawley, Laurie Dahl, Comfort Debrah, Neil Everitt, Chris Fidler, James Gill, James Harper, Marc Harrington, Matt Lawrence, Gordon Law, Andy Lee, Sami Mokbel, Graham Moody, Tyrone Reid, Joe O'Shea, Stuart Pink, Andy Sherwood, Bernie Trussler, Daniel Trussler, Lou Turner, Nick Veevers, Cat Winsor and Mark Winsor.

Neil McSteen – September 2008

FOREWORD BY MATT LAWRENCE

When the offer to join Crystal Palace came my way, I jumped at the chance. Here was an opportunity to play for a football club steeped in tradition. As a kid I remember Vince Hilaire flying down the wing, afro billowing in the air, bedecked in the same strip being worn this season. Then from the next chapter in my memory bank came the glory years of the Wright and Bright era: two names that brought Crystal Palace FC to the lips of many a neutral observer; myself included.

When the chance arose to write the foreword for Neil's book I agreed immediately. Then I remembered that I knew very little about the history of Crystal Palace, and was I really the write (yes, I know) man for the job. It was time to call in the big guns. My father and grandparents grew up in the Eagles territory of Thornton Heath. My father went to Selhurst Grammar, and watched his first games of football at Selhurst Park.

Unfortunately, the overriding memory of his younger years was Dennis Uphill missing from two yards in the early 60s. Maybe that's just the Alzheimer's kicking in!

Having been at Palace now for just over two years I've been lucky enough to work for Peter Taylor, Palace legend extraordinaire, and Neil Warnock – Palace legend of the future? We all hope so.

Last year, success on the pitch was a couple of coats of paint away. Hopefully, in the years to come, that success can be achieved, and Palace can rightfully return to the Premiership. Then maybe names such as Moses, Watson and Speroni can sit proudly alongside the names of Wright, Lombardo and Martyn that feature so prominently in Neil's book.

I hope you enjoy this book as much as I'm enjoying playing for your club. And here's to Neil having to compile chapters on life in the Premiership in future years.

Matt Lawrence – September 2008

INTRODUCTION

Crystal Palace On This Day is a full year's worth of facts, figures, highlights and lowlights from the club we all love.

Some you will know, some you won't, and some you'll wish you were never reminded about (yes, the 9-0 is in here) but the point is simple; all these events, matches, scorelines and off the pitch scandals make up the unique and wonderful club that is Crystal Palace.

We all know that following Palace is never boring, for even Trevor Francis and all his mid-table finishes was able to give us the legendary 5-0 mauling of Brighton & Hove Albion. Relegations, promotions and colourful chairmen, the Eagles never fail to deliver drama, emotion and occasionally a free-flowing passing move that results in a beautiful goal rather than a raised offside flag. I've done my best to cover many key events in the life of our club from 1905 onwards, and also to include some, quite frankly, bizarre incidents. The Mark Goldberg era undoubtedly provides a lot of these!

But writing this book has once again opened my eyes to how important Crystal Palace is as a football club, and how we should all still be immensely proud of what the club has achieved, and stands for. Looking back on the administration era after a period of relative stability, you get a sense of how close we came to extinction, so thank you Simon Jordan.

As we enter another uncertain period in the history of Palace, we should be acutely aware of how important this club was, is and will be to the people of South London and the surrounding area. Any prospective new owner should read this book to get an idea of what they are buying into.

So please do enjoy this book, because as a fellow Palace fan I know you have impeccable taste, a great sense of humour and a willingness to read numerous entries about missed titles and relegations alongside triumphant promotions and 5-0 victories over Manchester United in the top flight.

Neil McSteen – September 2008

CRYSTAL PALACE
On This Day

JANUARY

SATURDAY 1st JANUARY 1966

Steve Kember made his league debut against Bristol City aged just 17 years and 24 days, making him the fifth youngest player to appear for Palace.

FRIDAY 1st JANUARY 1937

After six months away from Selhurst Park, Tom Bromilow was reinstated as Crystal Palace manager following the resignation of R S Moyes and the advent of a settled boardroom.

THURSDAY 1st JANUARY 1981

Clive Allen was placed on the transfer list and dropped ahead of the trip to Maine Road to face Manchester City in the third round of the FA Cup.

FRIDAY 2nd JANUARY 1981

The day before a crucial FA Cup tie away to Manchester City, Malcolm Allison failed to show for the coach journey up north. The players hadn't seen him all week and were astonished when they saw the gaffer for the first time the next day... on *Football Focus* explaining how Palace were going to win the game! Needless to say, Allison picked a strange looking side that got beat 4-0.

MONDAY 2nd JANUARY 1989

Mark Bright scored the first of three hat-tricks he would hit in his Palace career when his trio of goals helped the Eagles to a 4-0 win over Walsall in a Division Two fixture.

MONDAY 3rd JANUARY 1966

After a series of rows with his players and with two years left on his contract, Palace manager Dick Graham was informed by the board that "we have had a meeting and we think you had better call it a day". Graham had been one of the first managers in the land to deploy a defence featuring twin centre-backs, a squad system complete with rotation, and declined to use the traditional 1-11 numbering of his players in order to confuse the opposition as to who was playing in what position. Arthur Rowe was subsequently put in temporary charge.

SATURDAY 3RD JANUARY 1942

Palace revived memories of the 10-0 thrashing they handed out to Brighton in April 1940 by again sticking another ten past their south coast rivals in a London League wartime fixture at Selhurst Park.

TUESDAY 3RD JANUARY 1922

The freehold to the land that would become Palace's new ground was finally purchased for £2,570 by an agent called Mr Richardson on behalf of Crystal Palace Football Club. Lying as wasteland since the brick manufacturing company moved out, the legendary Archibald Leitch was commissioned to design Selhurst Park. Leitch had already worked on Craven Cottage, Stamford Bridge and White Hart Lane and was aiming big with his new project, stating that Palace would have the largest ground in London and the most modern in the country.

SATURDAY 3RD JANUARY 1976

Palace set up a plum fourth round FA Cup tie with Leeds United after they beat non-league Scarborough 2-1 at the Athletic Ground. The match also saw the first appearance of Malcolm Allison's famous fedora. Initially worn to keep the sun from his eyes, the headgear rapidly became iconic.

FRIDAY 4TH JANUARY 1991

Stan Collymore joined Crystal Palace from Stafford Rangers for £100,000. He would only make 25 appearances for the Eagles, scoring twice, before leaving for Southend United for £150,000.

FRIDAY 4TH JANUARY 2002

Palace coach Terry Bullivant revealed that his plans for the FA Cup third round match against Premiership side Newcastle United had been hampered by the freezing conditions but admitted: "We won't need a lot of preparation, as to play at St. James' Park is a big experience and everyone is up for it."

SATURDAY 4TH JANUARY 2003

In-form midfielder Tommy Black blasted two second-half goals to see Palace safely through to the fourth round of the FA Cup after an own-goal from Tony Popovic had seen the Eagles trailing 1-0 away at Blackpool.

SATURDAY 5TH JANUARY 1946

In the first FA Cup competition since its enforced lay-off due to World War II, Palace played out a dour 0-0 draw against QPR in the third round in front of 20,000 fans at Loftus Road. But, without a full league programme and in order to make some money for the impoverished clubs, the FA decided to make all the rounds, up to the semi-final, two legged affairs for the first and only time in the competition's history. Palace now had a second leg at Selhurst Park to look forward to. On news of the pairing with the West London outfit, Palace directors saw fit to finally complete the transfer of Freddie Kurz at a then club record fee of £5,000 since 'guest' players weren't allowed to play in FA Cup fixtures. Kurz had 'guested' regularly for the Glaziers in the wartime championships and had made such an impact that Palace fans had long been petitioning the board to buy him outright from Grimsby Town.

MONDAY 5TH JANUARY 1981

Malcolm Allison agreed to work on a week-to-week contract after failing to get a deal from Palace chairman Ray Bloye, who was known to be seeking a buyer for his shares in the club.

SATURDAY 6TH JANUARY 1990

Palace began their FA Cup campaign at home to Portsmouth, who had just parted company with manager John Gregory two days previously. A crowd of 12,644 witnessed Palace progress to the next round thanks to substitute Geoff Thomas cancelling out Pompey's opener before Andy Gray slotted home a last-minute penalty. The match programme for the afternoon featured a poster of a very young Gareth Southgate.

SATURDAY 6TH JANUARY 2007

Shefki Kuqi put Palace ahead after just eight minutes in the third round tie with Swindon Town in the FA Cup. Jobi McAnuff made the game safe in the 70th minute, before the Wiltshire men grabbed an 85th minute consolation.

WEDNESDAY 6TH JANUARY 1993

Substitute referee Gerald Ashby only gave the go-ahead for the Coca-Cola League Cup quarter-final tie with Chelsea twenty minutes before kick-off due to the torrential rain that had been falling across South London all afternoon. In front of the biggest gate of the season, 28,510, Chris Coleman, in his role as stand-in striker, put Palace in front. Pouncing on an under-hit Frank Sinclair back-pass, 'Cookie' just about poked the ball home as the heavy conditions took the pace off the ball as it rolled agonisingly over the line. Andy Townsend then equalised, but it was then the turn of the Coca-Cola Cup kids to steal the show. The 18-year-old George Ndah had Palace back in the lead, before 19-year-old Grant Watts, who used to stand on the terraces with his dad watching the Eagles, put the game beyond Ian Porterfield's men three minutes after the break when he made it 3-1.

SATURDAY 7TH JANUARY 1922

Second Division Palace travelled to Goodison Park to face First Division Everton in the first round proper of the FA Cup, and pulled off one of the biggest shocks the competition has ever seen by winning 6-0 in front of a crowd of 45,000. It should have been 10-0 though, as Palace had two goals disallowed for offside and two legitimate claims for penalties waved away.

SATURDAY 7TH JANUARY 2006

There was to be no giant-killing in the FA Cup third round at Selhurst Park as goals from Michael Hughes, Jobi McAnuff, Andrew Johnson and Dougie Freedman gave Palace a comfortable 4-1 win over Colin Calderwood's League Two play-off chasers Northampton Town.

SATURDAY 8TH JANUARY 1966

In only his second game for Palace, Steve Kember scored the only goal as the Glaziers beat Bury 1-0 at Selhurst Park. At 17 years and 31 days Kember is still the youngest-ever goalscorer for Crystal Palace.

SATURDAY 8TH JANUARY 1938

With Matt Busby in their side, First Division Liverpool visited Selhurst Park for the first time in a third round FA Cup tie. The Reds rarely threatened and Palace couldn't find a winner so it was off to Anfield for the replay.

SATURDAY 8TH JANUARY 1977

Third Division Crystal Palace travelled up to Anfield in the third round of the FA Cup to face the mighty Liverpool. Venables' men did an excellent job in front of 44,730, landing a replay after the match finished 0-0. Liverpool went on to win the First Division and European Cup that season.

THURSDAY 8TH JANUARY 1981

Wimbledon chairman Ron Noades entered the fray as he attempted to buy Crystal Palace. Owner Ray Bloye refuted his initial advance.

WEDNESDAY 9TH JANUARY 1946

Palace drew 0-0 with Queens Park Rangers at Selhurst Park in the second leg of their third round FA Cup tie. With the tie 0-0 on aggregate, a single-game replay was required.

SATURDAY 9TH JANUARY 1915

A solid showing of 18,000 hardy souls turned up at St Andrews to see Southern League Crystal Palace hold Birmingham City of the Football League to a 2-2 draw in the first round of the FA Cup.

SATURDAY 9TH JANUARY 1965

Cliff Holton scored a hat-trick as Palace beat Bury 5-1 at Selhurst Park in the third round of the FA Cup. Holton's previous three-goal haul for the Glaziers had been two years previously in the 8-1 demolition of Harwich & Parkeston in the first round of the FA Cup.

TUESDAY 10TH JANUARY 1989

Steve Coppell paid Northampton Town £200,000 for winger Eddie McGoldrick as he pushed for promotion to the top flight.

THURSDAY 10TH JANUARY 1991

The *Croydon Guardian* published its first-ever Crystal Palace match report detailing all the action of a 0-0 draw with Nottingham Forest in the FA Cup.

WEDNESDAY 10th JANUARY 2001

While their form in Division One was poor, Palace continued to do well in cup competitions and against Liverpool in the first leg of the League Cup semi-final Alan Smith's men secured a 2-1 win to take to Anfield. With striker Michael Owen missing chance after chance, it was left to Latvian striker Andrejs Rubins to open the scoring with a delightful 25-yard strike nine minutes into the second half. Clinton Morrison then doubled Palace's lead after 77 minutes, only for Vladimir Smicer to pull one back immediately. After the match, Morrison gave an interview only to find that his words had been twisted to suggest that he wanted to show Owen how to score goals after the England international had a particularly dire game.

TUESDAY 11th JANUARY 1977

Paul Hinshelwood put Palace 1-0 up against Liverpool after seventeen minutes in the FA Cup third round replay, only for Kevin Keegan to equalise three minutes later. It was not until the 66th minute that Bob Paisley's men took the lead through Steve Heighway, who then made sure of Liverpool's progress by scoring again in the 72nd minute. George Graham grabbed a consolation strike two minutes from time as Venables' men put on a credible display in front of 42,664 fans at Selhurst Park against a team who would reach the final.

SATURDAY 12th JANUARY 1963

Palace followed up their last league game, a 3-0 home win over Millwall, with maximum points away at Brighton & Hove Albion: a 2-1 win. The back-to-back victories over the local rivals kick-started Palace's climb away from the foot of the Third Division.

WEDNESDAY 12th JANUARY 1938

In an FA Cup third round replay, Palace took the lead at Anfield against First Division Liverpool, only for the home side to score three without reply to win the tie. After the game, the Reds were forced to apologise by the FA for disparaging comments about Palace that appeared in the match programme.

SATURDAY 12TH JANUARY 1924

A good crowd of 17,000 turned up at The Nest to see Second Division Palace beat top-flight Tottenham Hotspur 2-0 in the first round of the FA Cup. Billy Morgan, a £500 signing from Coventry, plundered both goals from close range.

SATURDAY 12TH JANUARY 1907

The first round of the FA Cup saw Palace land an extremely tricky away tie at St James' Park against the reigning Football League champions, Newcastle United. The Magpies had also reached the previous season's FA Cup final and should have been too much for a Palace side with just four months' experience in the senior division of the Southern League. But just before half-time, Horace Astley tucked home past Newcastle keeper Jimmy Lawrence, one of several internationals in the home side's starting line-up, with what would be the only goal of the match. Newcastle had been unbeaten at home for over a year and would go on to win the league, yet lowly Palace had snatched an FAmous victory.

WEDNESDAY 13TH JANUARY 1915

Having secured a 2-2 draw away at St Andrews to earn a second chance against Birmingham City in the first round of the FA Cup, the directors of Crystal Palace took the unique decision to forgo home advantage and accept Birmingham's offer of hosting the replay. The decision caused great controversy at the time and was widely condemned, but with World War I in full progress in continental Europe attendances at Palace home games had declined sharply. Quite simply, club administrators needed the extra money that a larger crowd at St Andrews could provide. The game itself remained goalless until extra time, when Birmingham then turned on the class and put three past Palace to guarantee progress to the next round.

FRIDAY 13TH JANUARY 1995

Northern Ireland international Iain Dowie joined the Palace when Alan Smith paid £400,000 to sign the striker from Southampton.

THURSDAY 14TH JANUARY 1988

Steve Coppell signed Leyton-born England under-21 goalkeeper Perry Suckling from Manchester City for £100,000 to replace George Wood who left for Cardiff City on a free transfer. Suckling originally tried out at Palace as a schoolboy before joining his first club, Coventry City.

MONDAY 14TH JANUARY 2008

Popular defender Leon Cort finally moved to Stoke City in a £1.25 million transfer. Manager Neil Warnock didn't fancy him in his team as he didn't pick up enough yellow cards for his liking!

SATURDAY 15TH JANUARY 1972

A third round FA Cup-tie between Palace and Everton turned into a nasty affair after Joe Royle clattered keeper John Jackson. An ill-tempered game saw two pitch invasions and a 2-2 draw meant a replay at Goodison Park.

THURSDAY 15TH JANUARY 1998

Palace smashed their transfer record when they brought in French under-21 central defender Valerien Ismael from RC Strasbourg for £2.75 million. Tomas Brolin also signed, joining from Leeds on a free transfer until the end of the season.

FRIDAY 15TH JANUARY 1999

At 8pm an official announcement from Palace stated that Terry Venables was not going to continue in a coaching role and would, in future, be with the club on a consultancy basis only. Dave Butler and Terry Fenwick also departed from the coaching side. It was also confirmed that Steve Coppell would take over as manager, and John Cartwright the coaching, until the end of the season at least.

WEDNESDAY 16TH JANUARY 1946

Palace lost 1-0 to Queens Park Rangers in an FA Cup third round replay – after their initial two-legged tie ended goalless – and were dumped out of the competition. Whilst the game should have been played at Loftus Road, a frozen Craven Cottage was instead used to host the fixture.

SATURDAY 16TH JANUARY 1909

Palace found themselves drawn away in the first round of the FA Cup against none other than the cup-holders themselves, Wolverhampton Wanderers. A credible 2-2 draw took the tie to a replay.

TUESDAY 16TH JANUARY 1996

Palace were dumped out of the FA Cup in a third round replay against Port Vale, losing 4-3 after extra time. Gareth Taylor got only his second goal for Palace in the gathering mist and gloom at Vale Park, at the goal further from the travelling fans. This prompted a number of ironic T-shirts to be made up bearing the legend: "I saw Taylor score".

SATURDAY 16TH JANUARY 1996

With the media portraying Crystal Palace as a club in crisis off the pitch thanks to Mark Goldberg's financial problems, Attilio Lombardo played his last game for the club helping the Eagles battle back from 2-0 down against Stockport County to gain a point in front of 15,517 fans at Selhurst Park.

SATURDAY 17TH JANUARY 1981

Just 15,080 turned up at Selhurst Park to witness what would turn out to be Malcolm Allison's last game in charge of Palace, a 0-0 draw against Wolves in the First Division.

MONDAY 18TH JANUARY 1999

Cash-strapped Palace were given a shot in the arm when Brian Kidd shelled out £4.1m to add Matt Jansen to his already impressive collection of forwards at Blackburn Rovers. Jansen, who turned down Manchester United in favour of the Eagles, scored 11 goals in 33 appearances during his time at Selhurst Park.

FRIDAY 18TH JANUARY 2002

Manager Steve Kember, in a press conference ahead of the visit by Rotherham United in the league on the Saturday, was beginning to feel he had turned a corner: "We've had three good league wins on the trot and we are starting to do what we all said we'd do."

THURSDAY 21st JANUARY 1909

Palace knocked out the FA Cup holders Wolves in a pulsating replay that saw the tie go to extra time after the Midlands side made it 2-2 eight minutes from the end of normal time. Jimmy Bauchop put Palace 3-2 ahead before Archie Needham made the victory certain with what is regarded as one of Palace's finest ever goals. Receiving the ball inside his own half, Needham evaded numerous tackles as he ran at Wolves before lashing home from inside the box.

WEDNESDAY 21st JANUARY 1981

Ron Noades outlined his plans for Crystal Palace, but the deal was not yet complete as Ray Bloye was still in charge.

THURSDAY 22nd JANUARY 1981

Ray Bloye insisted he was still in charge at Palace and that he wouldn't be leaving in order to protect his staff and players. He also optimistically added that manager Malcolm Allison was safe until the end of the season.

MONDAY 22nd JANUARY 1996

Palace snapped up veteran defender Andy Linighan from Arsenal for a bargain £100,000.

FRIDAY 23rd JANUARY 1981

Ron Noades finally signed the deal that gave him ownership of Crystal Palace Football Club.

SATURDAY 24th JANUARY 1976

Third Division Palace travelled to Elland Road in the fourth round of the FA Cup to face a Leeds United team who were sitting third in the top flight – and had been runners-up to Bayern Munich in the European Cup just the season before. "We'll give them the fright of their lives," proclaimed Malcolm Allison before the match and so it proved. Playing with a sweeper system, the Eagles were tactically too good for United – in front of 43,116 fans – and could have won 4-0. As it was, a Dave Swindlehurst header was enough to lead Palace to an FAmous 1-0 win and a place in the fifth round.

MONDAY 24TH JANUARY 1994

Alan Smith brought in Paul Stewart on loan from Liverpool. The swoop for the former England international forward soon proved to be an inspired piece of business.

WEDNESDAY 24TH JANUARY 2001

Palace failed to reach the League Cup final after they were hammered 5-0 in the second-leg of the semi-final away at Liverpool, ducking out of the competition 6-2 on aggregate to leave the 4,000 travelling fans a long journey back to South London. Clinton Morrison was given a rough time by the Kop after derogatory comments about Reds striker Michael Owen were attributed to him. Anfield boss Gerard Houllier had stoked the flames before the game by declaring: "I am grateful to Clinton for telling us how to score. We must have left our own instruction book behind when we went to Selhurst Park. Now we must try to take a lesson from Clinton in the second leg. I found his comments very amusing."

SATURDAY 25TH JANUARY 1969

After topping the table in the early part of the season, Palace slipped to sixth in the Second Division when they lost 2-1 at home to Blackpool, putting a massive dent in their promotion hopes.

WEDNESDAY 25TH JANUARY 1995

Title-chasing Manchester United visited Selhurst Park with Alan Smith's men gaining a credible 1-1 draw courtesy of Gareth Southgate's goal. But the result was somewhat overshadowed when Eric Cantona, having been sent off for aiming a kick at Richard Shaw, decided to launch a kung-fu kick at, and then trade punches with, an FAn in the main stand after receiving abuse as he walked down the touchline to the dressing room.

MONDAY 26TH JANUARY 1981

The new owner of Crystal Palace – Ron Noades – turned up to meet his staff. He promptly sacked Malcolm Allison, who had been in charge for just 55 days, and paid him off until the end of the season.

FRIDAY 26TH JANUARY 2001

Clinton Morrison warned that he may play for the Republic of Ireland if new England boss Sven Goran Eriksson didn't include him in his plans. The Palace striker revealed: "Mick McCarthy has contacted me and says he wants me there – so I will have to see what England are saying and then decide. Ireland have a friendly coming up, so it will be a hard decision. I will have to sit down and think about it. I have my heart set on Ireland or England. I would dearly like to play for England, but it is a hard decision to make at the moment."

SATURDAY 27TH JANUARY 1934

Palace faced Arsenal in the fourth round of the FA Cup at Highbury, and although they lost 7-0, the 56,000 fans that turned up set a new record for the biggest-ever crowd to watch a Palace game, which lasted until Palace reached the FA Cup final in 1990.

TUESDAY 27TH JANUARY 1981

Dario Gradi was reunited with his former chairman when he left Wimbledon to become the new manager of Crystal Palace, calling in Mike Kelly as his assistant. In the process, Gradi became Palace's sixteenth post-war manager and the fourth in three turbulent months at Selhurst Park.

WEDNESDAY 27TH JANUARY 1999

Chairman Mark Goldberg and managing director Phil Alexander attended a meeting of the Palace Independent Supporters' Association in Croydon to face questions from the fans increasingly concerned at the perilous financial position of the club. Goldberg promised supporters he will clear Palace's £4m debt by May.

SATURDAY 27TH JANUARY 1990

Palace slipped into the fifth round of the FA Cup after hammering Huddersfield Town 4-0 in front of 12,920 fans at Selhurst Park.

FRIDAY 28TH JANUARY 2000

Swedish international striker Matt Svensson was transferred for a cut-price £600,000 to neighbours Charlton Athletic in a move that infuriated Palace fans tired of seeing their best assets sold off to keep the club afloat.

SATURDAY 28TH JANUARY 2006

Palace faced Preston North End at Deepdale twice in four days; the first encounter being a fourth round FA Cup tie. England international Andy Johnson opened the scoring for the Eagles before Brian O'Neill pegged Palace back to ensure a replay for the home side.

SATURDAY 29TH JANUARY 1916

Palace beat Croydon Common 2-0 at The Nest in Selhurst in a friendly which raised money for the War Comforts Fund.

SATURDAY 29TH JANUARY 1983

An Ian Edwards goal was enough to knock top-flight Birmingham City out of the FA Cup at the fourth round stage and send Second Division Palace through instead.

SATURDAY 30TH JANUARY 1926

A new record for gate receipts was set when Chelsea visited the recently opened Selhurst Park in the fourth round of the FA Cup. The attendance of 41,000 – who paid a total of £2,545 – wasn't bettered for nearly 40 years and saw Palace run out 2-1 winners thanks to Percy Cherrett and Alf Hawkins. Cherrett would go on to score 33 league and cup goals that season, the fifth highest total ever for a Palace player.

SATURDAY 31ST JANUARY 1981

Dario Gradi's first game in charge was a shocker as transfer-listed Clive Allen missed a penalty and both Jim Cannon and Tony Sealy were sent off as Palace crashed to a 2-0 defeat away to Middlesbrough in the First Division.

SATURDAY 31ST JANUARY 2004

Sections of the Arthur Wait Stand roof were torn off by high winds at Selhurst Park, delaying the kick-off by 45 minutes. When the Division One fixture against Wimbledon did start, Palace brushed their ex-tenants aside 3-1 thanks to a brace from Andy Johnson and a strike from Danny Granville. Future Palace star Jobi McAnuff notched for the visitors, who would change their name to MK Dons the following season.

CRYSTAL PALACE
On This Day

FEBRUARY

SATURDAY 1st FEBRUARY 1947

German prisoners-of-war were made to clear snow from the Selhurst Park pitch in order for a league fixture against Leyton Orient to take place. Palace then beat the East Londoners 2-0.

SATURDAY 1st FEBRUARY 1981

Player-coach Gerry Francis returned to QPR for a paltry £150,000, Palace having paid £465,000 for him in July 1979.

TUESDAY 1st FEBRUARY 2005

Palace drew a pulsating Premiership clash 2-2 at West Bromwich Albion thanks to an injury-time equaliser from Aki Riihilahti, coming moments after the Baggies thought they had won it through Robert Earnshaw.

SATURDAY 2nd FEBRUARY 2002

Crystal Palace scored three goals in six minutes to beat Sheffield Wednesday 3-1 in the league at Hillsborough, which pushed the Eagles up to fifth in the table. The goals came from Clinton Morrison (30), Dougie Freedman (35) and Jamie Smith (37) with loanee Sean Murphy from Sheffield United making his debut after signing the night before. Manager Trevor Francis said at the time, "We had to adapt to different conditions this afternoon and it was particularly pleasing to see the way we defended the lead."

FRIDAY 3rd FEBRUARY 2006

The FAI shortlisted three goals for the 2005 Republic of Ireland International Goal of the Year competition. Crystal Palace striker Clinton Morrison was nominated for two of the three strikes; his goals against Israel in a World Cup qualifier, and China in a friendly, both made the shortlist.

MONDAY 4th FEBRUARY 1928

George Clarke scored a hat-trick against Bournemouth as Crystal Palace won their Division Three (South) fixture 6-1. Clarke would score 22 goals by the end of the season from his position at outside left.

MONDAY 4th FEBRUARY 2002

Legendary boss Bert Head died from a stroke aged 85. Club historian at the time, Reverend Nigel Sands, said, "He was unquestionably one of the most likeable men ever to be associated with Crystal Palace FC."

WEDNESDAY 5TH FEBRUARY 1997

Steve Kember and the Crystal Palace reserve side failed to make it down to the West Country for a Combination game against Bristol Rovers when the petrol cap couldn't be removed from their coach after they stopped for fuel, despite everyone's best efforts. The team were stranded on the motorway, the match was postponed and Palace were fined for non-arrival at the venue.

TUESDAY 5TH FEBRUARY 2002

Crystal Palace announced the signing of striker Ade Akinbiyi from Leicester City for £2.4 million. Simon Jordan remarked: "Ade is a player I am very excited about and I am sure he will fly with this club."

WEDNESDAY 5TH FEB 2003

Following a 0-0 draw at Selhurst Park, Crystal Palace faced Premiership Liverpool in an FA Cup fourth round replay at Anfield. The Championship side played most of the second half with just ten men following Dougie Freedman's sending-off, but Trevor Francis' men pulled off a remarkable 2-0 victory thanks to Julian Gray and an own goal from Stephane Henchoz.

SATURDAY 6TH FEBRUARY 1915

Crystal Palace played their last ever game at *the* Crystal Palace; a Southern League fixture against Reading. The Admiralty requisitioned the stadium soon after for the war effort.

SATURDAY 6TH FEBRUARY 1937

Bob Bigg put three past Exeter City as Crystal Palace cruised to an 8-0 victory in Division Three (South). Croydon-born Bigg went on to score 41 goals in 114 appearances.

SATURDAY 6TH FEBRUARY 1943

Arsenal put nine past Crystal Palace without reply on their way to winning the Football League South.

TUESDAY 7TH FEBRUARY 2006

Crystal Palace lost 2-1 in an FA Cup fourth round replay at home to Preston North End with Danielle Dichio's brace too much for Darren Wards' first-half opener. Only 7,356 turned up for the 'entertainment'.

WEDNESDAY 8TH FEBRUARY 1961

Johnny Byrne gained the first of his seven England under-23 caps when he featured against Wales in a 2-0 victory at Goodison Park.

THURSDAY 8TH FEBRUARY 1996

Dave Bassett came in as manager at Crystal Palace after the Eagles' promotion drive had come unstuck in the preceding weeks. Steve Coppell remained 'upstairs' as 'Technical Director'.

MONDAY 9TH FEBRUARY 1981

Fans lobbied the Football League after learning of Ron Noades' ground-sharing scheme with Wimbledon.

WEDNESDAY 10TH FEBRUARY 1915

Crystal Palace was closed entirely to the public having been commandeered by the Admiralty to be used as Royal Naval Shore Station HMS Victory VI during World War I. Over 125,000 men were trained for war service in the grounds. Crystal Palace, meanwhile, had their fixtures unceremoniously cancelled and had to find a new home. Millwall and Croydon Common offered Palace a temporary base but the directors plumped to become tenants of amateur outfit West Norwood at their small Herne Hill home.

SATURDAY 11TH FEBRUARY 1950

Crystal Palace recorded their biggest win of the season when they beat Brighton & Hove Albion 6-0 in the league at Selhurst Park. Player-manager Ronnie Rooke displayed some of the skills that made him the First Division's top scorer with Arsenal just two seasons previously when he completed his hat-trick with 15 minutes still to go. The 38-year-old would finish as Palace's top league goalscorer for the season with 21 strikes from 39 appearances.

SATURDAY 11TH FEBRUARY 1939

A top-of-the-table clash between Crystal Palace and Monmouthshire outfit Newport County attracted a healthy 30,000 crowd to Selhurst Park. Palace took a second-half lead but could not close the game down, allowing County to sneak an equaliser three minutes from time. County eventually won the league, with Palace finishing runners-up again, three points adrift.

SUNDAY 12TH FEBRUARY 1984

Alan Mullery made his best signing for Crystal Palace when he bought Phil Barber from non-league Aylesbury Town for £7,500. 'Mr 110%' was initially signed as a striker but later featured in midfield.

TUESDAY 12TH FEBRUARY 2008

Crystal Palace USA announced their move to the UMBC Stadium in Catonsville, five miles south of downtown Baltimore.

TUESDAY 12TH FEBRUARY 2002

The funeral of former manager Bert Head took place at Reading Crematorium with Cliff Jackson, Steve Kember, Bobby Woodruff, Mel Blyth and David Payne – who all played under him – present alongside club chaplain, the Reverend Nigel Sands.

MONDAY 13TH FEBRUARY 1961

Johnny Byrne captained the Army under-23s as they took on their Scottish counterparts at Fir Park, Motherwell. The Army team included a number of notable Scots, including the legendary Jim Baxter of Rangers.

FRIDAY 13TH FEBRUARY 1998

Attilio Lombardo and Michele Padovano both distanced themselves from press reports that quoted the pair attacking Crystal Palace's Mitcham training ground and the club's lack of medical staff. The pair admitted to being frustrated that they could not help the Eagles out of their dire predicament due to injuries sustained in December.

SATURDAY 14TH FEBRUARY 1948

Belgian Marcel Gaillard became the first player from outside the British Isles to play for Palace when he started against Watford at Vicarage Road. Gaillard, who moved to Portsmouth in 1951, was also the first overseas player to score for Palace, scoring in the 5-0 romp.

SATURDAY 14TH FEBRUARY 1976

Palace donned a new kit, all white with a red and blue diagonal sash, for their visit to Stamford Bridge in the fifth round of the FA Cup. A crowd of 54,407 watched in awe as Peter Taylor tore Second Division Chelsea apart as the Eagles triumphed 3-2.

SATURDAY 14TH FEBRUARY 2003

Andy Johnson made it 18 goals in 16 games with a first-half hat-trick against Stoke City as Crystal Palace romped to a 6-3 win that edged them closer to the play-offs. It was the first time since Christmas 1961 that nine goals have been seen in a league game at Selhurst Park.

TUESDAY 15TH FEBRUARY 1967

Johnny Byrne returned to Crystal Palace from West Ham for £45,000 following Bert Head's negotiations with the former England man during a train journey back from the north of England after the Palace and West Ham teams found themselves on the same service.

SUNDAY 15TH FEBRUARY 1998

It was an all-Premiership affair at Highbury in the fifth round of the FA Cup as Crystal Palace took on Arsenal, minus the injured Ian Wright. Chances were at a premium for the Eagles, who should have had a penalty just before the break when Gunners keeper Alex Manninger crashed into Jamie Fullarton a yard inside the box, only for referee Martin Bodenham to give a free-kick outside the area. Dennis Bergkamp and Nicolas Anelka both went close for the home side, but the 37,164 crowd had to make do with a dour 0-0 and a replay.

TUESDAY 16TH FEBRUARY 1982

Progress in the league might have been frustrating, but Palace impressed in the FA Cup when a 1-0 replay win over Orient set up a tasty quarter-final tie with Terry Venables' QPR and half the team that represented the Eagles in the top flight the season before!

SUNDAY 16TH FEBRUARY 2003

Terry Venables' Leeds United visited Selhurst Park for a fourth round FA Cup tie, but Palace didn't progress to the next round even though Tommy Black had an effort that clearly went over the line, as proved by the Sky TV cameras present, but the goal was not given. Leeds eventually won 2-1.

TUESDAY 17TH FEBRUARY 1981

Ray Bloye officially stepped down as the Crystal Palace chairman and Ron Noades was duly elected to the role.

ANDREW JOHNSON

SATURDAY 17TH FEBRUARY 1990

Phil Barber was the hero when Crystal Palace booked their berth in the FA Cup quarter-finals after they beat Rochdale 1-0 at Selhurst Park in front of 17,044.

MONDAY 18TH FEBRUARY 1924

After three goalless draws against First Division Notts County, the fourth game in the second round of the FA Cup finally produced a positive result when Crystal Palace won 2-1 at the neutral Villa Park.

WEDNESDAY 18TH FEBRUARY 1981

Ron Noades stated publicly that he has killed off the idea of ground-sharing with Wimbledon.

SATURDAY 19TH FEBRUARY 1994

Islington-born Damian Matthew got on the scoresheet as Crystal Palace claimed a useful 1-1 draw away to Nottingham Forest in the Championship. A crowd of 24,232 were in attendance at the City Ground.

SATURDAY 19TH FEBRUARY 2000

In the battle of the basement strugglers, Crystal Palace came off second best to Nottingham Forest when they lost 2-0 at the City Ground in front of 16,421. Alan Rogers and Nigel Quashie were on target for David Platt's men, but Dougie Freedman also went close for the East Midlanders in the dying moments of the match.

SATURDAY 20TH FEBRUARY 1965

Second Division Crystal Palace progressed to the last eight of the FA Cup for the first time since 1907 after beating top-flight Nottingham Forest 3-1 in front of a then record crowd of 41,667 at a snowy Selhurst Park.

SATURDAY 20TH FEBRUARY 1926

After defeating Chelsea in the fourth round, Third Division (South) Crystal Palace were handed a fifth round home tie with top-flight Manchester City. Palace put four past City, but the Maine Road outfit scored an incredible eleven goals! City eventually reached the final, but lost 1-0 to Bolton Wanderers. The whole of the 1925/26 season saw a number of high-scoring matches; this was put down to changes in the offside law.

FRIDAY 20TH FEBRUARY 1998

Palace chairman Ron Noades held open discussions with Mark Goldberg regarding the possible purchase of the club, with both sides reporting a satisfactory meeting. Steve Coppell confirmed an interest in Sasa Curcic and Newcastle United's Temuri Ketsbaia but refuted suggestions that he will be sacked if a takeover occurs at the club.

SATURDAY 21ST FEBRUARY 1998

Palace travelled to Highbury for the second time in less than a week, having faced the Gunners in the FA Cup the previous Sunday. This time, Steve Coppell's men were on the hunt for Premiership points, and with Arsene Wenger having nine first team players out due to a midweek bout of flu, the Eagles fancied their chances. But, it wasn't to be as Gilles Grimandi scored the only goal of the game to send Arsenal second in the league. The majority of the 38,094 crowd went home happy but slightly bemused that referee Jeff Winter had managed to dish out seven yellow cards in what wasn't a dirty game.

SATURDAY 22ND FEBRUARY 1969

After nearly a month without football due to the harsh weather, the Second Division resumed. The break seemed to have done Palace good, as they beat Hull City 2-0 at Selhurst and did not lose another match until they were promoted.

SATURDAY 22ND FEBRUARY 1913

A huge 44,500 crowd turned up at Villa Park to watch top-flight Aston Villa put five goals past Palace without reply in the third round of the FA Cup. Charlie Wallace, who played for Palace from 1905-1907, turned out for the Birmingham side who eventually went on to lift the famous cup in front of 120,000 at the Crystal Palace. Incidentally, it was the first competitive meeting against the team that inspired the formation of Crystal Palace as a club in 1905, Edmund Goodman having left Aston Villa to help organise the new Crystal Palace FC off and on the pitch.

TUESDAY 22ND FEBRUARY 1983

Crystal Palace beat Bolton Wanderers 3-0 at home in the league but a pitiful crowd of only 4,456 was lost in the expanse of Selhurst Park as the fans' backlash against the appointment of Alan Mullery really started to bite.

SATURDAY 23RD FEBRUARY 1924

After beating top-flight opponents in the shape of Spurs and Notts County, Crystal Palace were drawn at home to Third Division (South) Swindon Town in the third round of the FA Cup. In what proved to be their last game at The Nest ahead of the move to Selhurst Park, Palace contrived to lose 2-1.

WEDNESDAY 23RD FEBRUARY 2000

Crystal Palace midfielder Craig Foster came on as a 64th minute substitute for Australia as they beat Hungary 3-0 in a friendly match in Budapest. Former Eagles Kevin Muscat and Craig Moore, who scored the third, both started for the Socceroos.

MONDAY 24TH FEBRUARY 1997

Crystal Palace received planning permission to rebuild the Main Stand and transform it into a 7,750 two-tier structure featuring executive boxes. Ron Noades stated; "Hopefully, we can get everything in place to start the new millennium with the new stand fully constructed". Speculation increased that England would win the bid to host the 2006 World Cup, and the possibility of Selhurst Park being confirmed as one of the venues increased with the rebuilding news.

TUESDAY 25TH FEBRUARY 1919

Not only was Edmund Goodman the manager of Crystal Palace, he was also the club secretary. Club minutes recorded that on this day Goodman himself set the ball rolling on acquiring a better stadium than The Nest when he contacted Mr Allen of the London, Brighton & South Coast Railway with regards to getting the freehold on the land that would host Selhurst Park.

SATURDAY 25TH FEBRUARY 1933

Peter Simpson banged home his second ever hat-trick for Crystal Palace in the 4-1 rout of Cardiff City at Selhurst Park in Division Three (South).

WEDNESDAY 25TH FEBRUARY 1998

In the early hours of the morning, Mark Goldberg and Ron Noades exchanged contracts on the £30m sale of Crystal Palace Football Club to the Bromley-based businessman. The purchase was made in instalments and infamously did not actually include ownership of Selhurst Park which Noades managed to keep for himself. As part of the deal, Noades stayed on as club chairman until October when the final part of the deal was completed. Goldberg also hinted at managerial changes throughout the club and met with Steve Coppell to discuss a new role of Technical Director of Football for the Palace manager.

THURSDAY 26TH FEBRUARY 1998

In the wake of the Goldberg-Noades deal, the press claimed Terry Venables was set to be named Crystal Palace's new manager, with Steve Coppell willingly moving upstairs. Coppell denied this, claiming he was still very much the boss at Crystal Palace and working for the club's owner, who was still Ron Noades

FRIDAY 26TH FEBRUARY 1999

Crystal Palace failed to pay the wages of both players and staff, but chairman Mark Goldberg stated that he would pay them out his own pocket in five days time.

FRIDAY 26TH FEBRUARY 2000

Left-back Ashley Cole, on loan from Arsenal, and striker Mikael Forssell, on loan from Chelsea, both made their debuts for Crystal Palace in a 1-0 defeat away to Grimsby, watched by 5,421 at Blundell Park. Australian forward Nicky Rizzo also made a rare start for the Eagles in this game.

MONDAY 27TH FEBRUARY 1989

Crystal Palace assistant manager Ian Evans departed suddenly to take charge of Swansea City after Terry Yorath left to join Bradford City following the dismissal of manager Terry Dolan and his coaching staff, including Stan Ternent. It was the first change in the coaching and managerial staff in over four-and-a-half years which was something of an achievement considering all the previous comings and goings.

THURSDAY 27TH FEBRUARY 1997

After being approached by Manchester City, following Steve Coppell's departure – and turning them down after being given a pay-rise by chairman Ron Noades – Dave Bassett shocked Crystal Palace once more when he walked out to become manager of Premiership strugglers Nottingham Forest. Bassett claimed he left to further his career and to be nearer his Sheffield home.

FRIDAY 27TH FEBRUARY 1998

Mark Goldberg confirmed he would meet Terry Venables on the Monday to discuss the Australian coach's future. The new owner of Crystal Palace also stated that he wanted to increase the capacity of Selhurst Park to 40,000 and that he had a "five year plan to achieve the status of a club that can compete in Europe". On the pitch, Palace hadn't won in the league since the 1-0 victory over Spurs in November.

MONDAY 28TH FEBRUARY 1983

Alan Mullery narrowly missed out on taking Crystal Palace into the quarter-finals of the FA Cup after Burnley won a fifth round replay at Turf Moor 1-0 thanks to twice-taken penalty.

FRIDAY 28TH FEBRUARY 1997

At 1pm Ron Noades held a press conference to introduce Steve Coppell as the caretaker-manager until the end of the season. Coppell, who had been scouting for Palace after leaving the hot seat at Manchester City, expressed his delight at being back in charge of the Eagles: "I'm thrilled to be back at Palace once more."

SATURDAY 29TH FEBRUARY 1936

Scheduled to face Torquay United at home in the league, Crystal Palace were instead instructed to host Coventry City at short notice after the Football League suspended the published programme of matches and substituted other pairings due to wrangling with the Pools companies over their use of the League's fixtures for their games. Attendances everywhere were adversely affected, so by the time Torquay eventually came to Selhurst Park on the 14th March, the Football League had sensibly backed down.

CRYSTAL PALACE
On This Day

MARCH

MONDAY 1st MARCH 1926

Selhurst Park hosted its one and only full England international, when 23,000 turned up on a Monday afternoon for a friendly against Wales. Jack Fowler put the Welsh ahead in the 43rd minute, only for England to equalise through William Walker in the 54th minute. Len Davies then put Wales back in front just two minutes later before Fowler scored his second goal in the 57th minute to cap a memorable St David's day victory for the visitors. Making his debut that day for the home side was Willis Edwards, who in the process became the 500th player to be capped for England.

WEDNESDAY 1st MARCH 1989

Ahead of the fixture with Oxford United at the Manor Ground, Stan Ternent was introduced to the Crystal Palace squad as the replacement for the recently departed Ian Evans. As first team coach, Ternent would stay late after normal training to organise scoring contests for Mark Bright and Ian Wright in order to hone their competitiveness.

WEDNESDAY 2nd MARCH 1977

Vince Hilaire made his debut for Crystal Palace in a 3-2 defeat away to Lincoln in the Second Division.

TUESDAY 2nd MARCH 1999

Rumours abounded that Crystal Palace were to be placed into administration due to their chronic financial problems. Steve Coppell vowed to stay with the club whatever the outcome of the upheavals and against the backdrop of uncertainty he somehow inspired his men to a 1-1 draw that evening, away to Sheffield United in Division One.

SATURDAY 2nd MARCH 2002

Crystal Palace, unbeaten in their previous five away games, capitulated at Blundell Park, losing 5-2 to Grimsby Town in Division One with Julian Gray and Clinton Morrison the scorers for the Eagles. Trevor Francis commented: "I did not think it would have been possible to have a scoreline like this." Promotion-chasing Palace had previously beaten the Mariners 5-0 in the league in September.

SATURDAY 3RD MARCH 1962

Johnny Byrne played what proved to be his last game for Crystal Palace before signing for West Ham. It was not a great way to sign off, as the Glaziers lost 4-1 away to Peterborough United, slipping back to tenth in the table after topping it in September.

WEDNESDAY 3RD MARCH 1915

Crystal Palace played their first fixture as tenants at Herne Hill – home to amateur club West Norwood – having been forced to move from the Crystal Palace after the Admiralty's commandeering of the Sydenham Hill site. Southampton provided the opponents in a rearranged Southern League fixture, and just as the Saints won in Palace's first ever competitive match, the south coast team left South London victorious after a 2-1 win.

WEDNESDAY 3RD MARCH 1999

The morning started with Mark Goldberg suggesting that he had a new plan to beat Crystal Palace's financial crisis. But by the afternoon, Palace media manager Terry Byfield issued a press statement from the board confirming that the administrators had been called in to look at the financial affairs of the club.

SATURDAY 4TH MARCH 1961

Terry Long made his 214th consecutive league appearance for Crystal Palace in the 2-0 home victory over Gillingham, a record only surpassed by John Jackson who managed 222.

WEDNESDAY 4TH MARCH 1998

With a general lack of interest from other clubs in the Premiership, Palace confirmed their entry into the Uefa Inter-Toto Cup for the summer.

SATURDAY 4TH MARCH 2000

The Crystal Palace Supporters' Trust was officially launched ahead of the home game against Manchester City with the aim of raising £10m through donations and loans from fans in order to help bring the club out of administration. Steve Coppell gave his unswerving support to the initiative. The match itself attracted the best crowd of the season so far, as 21,052 turned up to see Clinton Morrison's 27th minute header cancel out Bob Taylor's eighth minute opener.

WEDNESDAY 5TH MARCH 1969

Crystal Palace faced a tough trip to the Baseball Ground to play Championship favourites and table-toppers Derby County in what, at the time, looked like a tough examination of their promotion credentials. Incredibly, the Glaziers had *five* goals ruled out for infringements before eventually prevailing over Brian Clough's men thanks to a Bobby Woodruff strike.

TUESDAY 5TH MARCH 2002

Crystal Palace drew 0-0 with Portsmouth in a Championship fixture in front of 15,915 at Selhurst Park.

SATURDAY 6TH MARCH 1976

Alan Whittle fired Crystal Palace into the semi-finals of the FA Cup for the very first time when his strikes settled the tie against Sunderland at Roker Park. A crowd of 53,850 bore witness to a tight game between the champions-elect of the Second Division, and Third Division Palace.

SATURDAY 6TH MARCH 1982

Crystal Palace faced eventual finalists QPR on the plastic at Loftus Road in the quarter-finals of the FA Cup. A Shepherd's Bush crowd of 24,653 – the biggest that the Eagles played in front of all season – were treated to a match strangely lacking in passion on the pitch, but not off it. Somewhat inevitably, ex-Palace striker Clive Allen won the game for Rangers with the only goal of the match three minutes from time, denying manager Steve Kember and the long-suffering Palace fans a place in the semi-finals.

WEDNESDAY 7TH MARCH 1962

Johnny Byrne completed his move to First Division West Ham United for a record fee between British clubs. The cash-plus-player exchange had Byrne valued at £58,000 with Ron Brett coming in at £7,000 as he moved back to Selhurst Park for a second spell. Byrne had it written into his contract that he was allowed to come back to play for Palace a month later in their showpiece friendly against the former champions of Europe, Real Madrid. The £65,000 deal was second only to Jimmy Greaves' £80,000 transfer from Chelsea to AC Milan.

SATURDAY 7TH MARCH 1908

Bill Davies became Crystal Palace's first ever international, receiving a cap for Wales when they took on Scotland in a British International Championship fixture in front of 18,000 at Dens Park, Dundee. Signed from Stoke City, the winger couldn't help his country avoid a 2-1 defeat.

TUESDAY 7TH MARCH 1995

Chris Armstrong became the first Premiership player to fail a drugs test and be suspended, having tested positive for cannabis.

THURSDAY 8TH MARCH 1962

Goalkeeper John Jackson signed his first professional contract with Crystal Palace, coming in as an understudy to Bill Glazier. The Hammersmith-born shot-stopper would go on to play 393 times for Palace, once playing 138 consecutive league matches.

FRIDAY 8TH MARCH 2002

Andrejs Rubins and Aleksandrs Kolinko received call-ups from the Latvian national side for their friendly against Luxembourg on Wednesday 27th March. Latvia won the game in Hesperange 3-0.

SATURDAY 9TH MARCH 1907

In only their second season, Crystal Palace reached the quarter-finals of the FA Cup. A record crowd of 35,000 turned up to see how Palace would fare against an Everton side with nine internationals on their books. Horace Astley put Palace ahead just before half-time, but the Toffees levelled on the hour. Neither team could score a winner, so the tie went to a replay.

THURSDAY 9TH MARCH 1978

Crystal Palace paid Aston Villa £40,000 for the services of keeper John Burridge. He had previously played at Southend United on loan.

THURSDAY 9TH MARCH 2000

Palace administrators were hopeful of a deal with Singaporean financier Gerry Lim to save the club. Steve Coppell knew little about his potential boss. "I've met him twice but I don't know any more about him than most people. He's been constant in his wanting to buy the club. We've had nobody else so I'm grateful. Just as long as he's got a big cheque book."

WEDNESDAY 10TH MARCH 1965

Crystal Palace failed to reach the semi-finals of the FA Cup when they lost to eventual finalists Leeds United 3-0 in front of 45,384 at Selhurst Park.

SATURDAY 10TH MARCH 1990

Crystal Palace booked their place in the semi-finals of the FA Cup for only the second time in their history after they won a scrappy encounter 1-0 against Cambridge United at a packed Abbey Stadium. Skipper Geoff Thomas got the all important goal in the 78th minute; a scuffed shot finding its way into the back of the net through a forest of legs.

THURSDAY 10TH MARCH 1994

Ilford-born Bruce Antonio Dyer made history when he became the first teenager in the English game to be transferred for seven figures when Alan Smith paid Watford £1.1m for his services. Dyer was given the number 11 shirt on arrival at Selhurst Park.

WEDNESDAY 11TH MARCH 1998

Crystal Palace were in deep relegation trouble following their seventh consecutive Premiership defeat when they were hammered 6-2 by Chelsea at Stamford Bridge. Hermann Hreidarsson did volley the Eagles into an early lead, but braces from Gianluca Vialli and Tore Andre Flo coupled with strikes from Gianfranco Zola and Dennis Wise saw Palace off. Marcus Bent netted a late consolation with his first goal for the Palace.

SATURDAY 12TH MARCH 1932

Peter Simpson reached a century of league goals in just his ninety-seventh game, as his hat-trick helped Palace to a 5-0 home win over Cardiff City. Typically, Palace then went and lost 5-0 the following week away to Northampton Town.

THURSDAY 12TH MARCH 1981

Selhurst Park saw a flurry of activity on transfer deadline day as Peter Nicholas moved to Arsenal for £500,000 and Tony Sealy joined Terry Venables at "Queens Park Palace" for £80,000. The somewhat disappointing incoming recruits were Tommy Langley from QPR for £120,000, David Price from Arsenal for £80,000 and Brian Bason from Plymouth, again for £80,000.

THURSDAY 13TH MARCH 1958

With Crystal Palace in trouble in the Third Division (South), manager Cyril Spiers made one last move to try to keep the Glaziers out of the forthcoming new Fourth Division when he signed inside-left Johnny Nichol from Chelsea, and immediately made him captain.

WEDNESDAY 13TH MARCH 1907

Crystal Palace headed to Goodison Park in an FA Cup quarter-final replay against Everton, but found themselves three down after half an hour, and eventually went down 4-0.

FRIDAY 13TH MARCH 1998

Mark Goldberg and Ron Noades took drastic action with Crystal Palace marooned to the bottom of the Premiership. Steve Coppell was moved upstairs when he formally accepted the role of Director of Football, and was replaced with immediate effect by Attilio Lombardo, with Tomas Brolin as his translator. The only English the former Juventus man actually knows are the profanities that David Tuttle has taught him. Lombardo likens the whole episode as like "being hit by a bus".

MONDAY 14TH MARCH 1921

Future Crystal Palace manager Tom Bromilow made his debut for England in a friendly against Wales at Ninian Park, Cardiff. Bromilow played left-half for Liverpool, having famously turned up asking for a trial having de-mobbed from the Army. After winning two titles with his local team, Bromilow moved into coaching in Holland before embarking on a managerial career with Burnley in 1932, ending up at Palace in July 1935.

SATURDAY 14TH MARCH 1981

Dario Gradi made it seven league games without a point following Crystal Palace's 1-0 defeat at home to Sunderland.

SATURDAY 14TH MARCH 1991

Crystal Palace took six points off Liverpool in the league as they completed their first ever double over the Reds, thanks to Eric Young slotting past Bruce Grobbelaar to give Steve Coppell's men a memorable 1-0 win. It was Palace's fourth win over Liverpool in their last five encounters.

SATURDAY 14TH MARCH 1998

A stunning Matt Jansen volley from 25 yards wasn't enough to give new manager Attilio Lombardo anything from his first game in charge as Crystal Palace crashed 3-1 to Aston Villa at Villa Park in the Premiership.

WEDNESDAY 15TH MARCH 1961

Johnny Byrne scored for his country in an under-23 international at White Hart Lane, as England beat West Germany 4-1. But it was his impressive work with wing-half partner Bobby Moore that really caught the eye, something that was not lost on Moore's manager at West Ham, Ron Greenwood.

SATURDAY 15TH MARCH 1958

Johnny McNichol scored on his debut against Port Vale as Crystal Palace claimed their first win in six games as they struggled to avoid the drop into the Fourth Division.

THURSDAY 15TH MARCH 2001

Play-off final hero David Hopkin returned to Selhurst Park in a £1.5m switch from Premiership Bradford City. Crystal Palace were in deep relegation trouble, and the Scot's presence helped bolster a fragile team. Hopkin would go on to play a significant hand in keeping the Eagles up!

MONDAY 16TH MARCH 1914

Left-back Horace Colclough became Crystal Palace's first-ever representative for the senior England team when he made his debut against Wales at Ninian Park. A crowd of 17,586 were present to see England score twice in the second half to record a 2-0 win. Born in Longton, Staffordshire, Colclough joined the Palace from Crewe Alexandra and could also play in the right-back berth.

TUESDAY 17TH MARCH 1987

Wimbledon-born Alan Pardew joined from Yeovil for a bargain £7,000.

WEDNESDAY 17TH MARCH 1999

A press conference at Selhurst Park heard Mark Goldberg and David Bucher of Bucher Philips explain the club was in administration. A debt of £22m was revealed; further cut-price sales of the club's players inevitably followed.

SATURDAY 18TH MARCH 1978

Workington-born keeper John Burridge made his debut for Crystal Palace in their home fixture against Brighton and kept a clean sheet. Shut-outs would become a feature of "Budgie's" career at Selhurst Park, for in the 1978/9 promotion season he would keep 21 clean sheets and concede only 24 goals; a club record that still stands in August 2008.

MONDAY 18TH MARCH 2002

Dougie Freedman was called up for the Scotland squad for their friendly against France on March 27th. France won the actual game 5-0 in front of 80,000 at the Stade De France. Freedman played in the first half before making way for Scot Gemmill in the 46th minute.

SATURDAY 19TH MARCH 2005

Crystal Palace faced future champions Chelsea at Stamford Bridge on a baking hot March afternoon. Frank Lampard put the Blues 1-0 up after 29 minutes but Aki Riihilahti equalised 13 minutes later to take the teams level going into the break. However, second-half goals from Joe Cole and late substitute Mateja Kezman (2) sealed three points for the hosts. It was not all bad news for Eagles fans, though, as England manager Sven-Goran Eriksson called up Andrew Johnson for his England squad later that night.

TUESDAY 20TH MARCH 1990

Ian Wright broke his leg for the second time in the season during the 1-1 draw with Derby County at Selhurst Park, Paul Blades having caught the Crystal Palace hitman in exactly the same spot where he had broken it previously. Matters were made worse for Wright when physio Dave West told him it was a double break.

SATURDAY 21ST MARCH 1953

William Simpson scored the only hat-trick of his Crystal Palace career when he single-handedly guided his team to a 3-0 win over Swindon at Selhurst Park in Division Three (South).

SATURDAY 21ST MARCH 1981

Dario Gradi got his first point as Crystal Palace manager when his men managed a 1-1 draw at Leicester City.

SATURDAY 22ND MARCH 2000

Crystal Palace headed back to Loftus Road for the first time since a 6-0 thrashing at the hands of QPR, a result that guaranteed Rangers' league status on the last day of the 1998/99 season. A degree of revenge was dished out as the Eagles left West London with three points thanks to Clinton Morrison's 68th-minute strike.

FRIDAY 22ND MARCH 2002

Following a recent run of results that had seen Palace's promotion push put back, manager Trevor Francis remarked: "I know some people have given up but in football the fight is not over till the fat lady sings."

MONDAY 23RD MARCH 1981

The Minnesota Kicks of the North American Soccer League (NASL) were the second American visitors to Selhurst Park and included former Palace player Stewart Jump in their team. The attendance was a pitiful 1,490 who witnessed a 1-1 draw. Alan Wiley put the transatlantic visitors 1-0 up, with Les Carter sparing the home side's blushes with a late equaliser. The match went to an old NASL-style 35-yard shoot-out to decide matters. Players had five seconds to dribble with the ball from the halfway line and beat the goalkeeper. Four of five Palace players scored, but Gerry Murphy missed, leaving the way for Jump to score the decisive goal for Minnesota.

SATURDAY 23RD MARCH 1996

There was controversy when Terry Fenwick brought his Portsmouth side to Selhurst Park. In front of 17,039, Palace midfielder Andy Roberts thought he had nicked a win in the dying seconds of the game when he lashed the ball into the net, only to turn around to see that the referee had blown his whistle for full-time as the ball left his boot.

SATURDAY 23RD MARCH 2002

A crowd of 21,038 witnessed a 2-0 home win over Walsall that kept Crystal Palace's faint play-off hopes alive. Clinton Morrison was first to net and Dougie Freedman added a second from the penalty spot – his 20th league goal for the season. With Morrison having reached that milestone earlier in March the duo were the first forward partnership since the halcyon days of Mark Bright and Ian Wright to reach such numbers.

SATURDAY 25TH MARCH 1922

Albert Harry, an outside-right who signed from amateur side Kingstonian after impressing Palace manager Edmund Goodman in a Surrey Charity Shield final at The Nest, scored a brace on his debut in the 4-1 trouncing of Bury. Harry, who learnt his skills with the British Army in India, would play for Palace for 12 years scoring 55 goals in 440 appearances.

TUESDAY 25TH MARCH 2003

Crystal Palace paid their first visit to the Withdean Stadium to face Brighton & Hove Albion in the league but not even Noel Whelan, on loan from Middlesbrough, could help the Eagles find a way through as the game finished 0-0.

FRIDAY 26TH MARCH 1999

Chairman Mark Goldberg stated that the club's wage bill had been reduced from £7.5m to £4.5m after the recent departure of players, and that further cuts would be needed in order to put the club back on a firm footing. As a sideshow to the chaos that Goldberg had got the club into, Sasa Curcic protested outside Downing Street about the NATO bombing attacks on his home city of Belgrade in Serbia.

MONDAY 27TH MARCH 1989

Ian Wright opened the scoring against Brighton & Hove Albion on Easter Monday with a sizzling shot from 20 yards – the goal was the 100th strike of the feared Wright/Bright partnership. Referee Kelvin Morton then created a Football League record when he awarded an astonishing five penalties in the match, but not before he sent off Albion's Mike Trusson for a foul on Eddie McGoldrick. The first of the spot kicks came in the 38th minute, which Mark Bright converted following a foul on himself to make it 2-0. But, before the interval, Crystal Palace were awarded two more which were missed by Bright and Wright, respectively. In the 65th minute, Albion won a spot kick that Alan Curbishley converted to halve the deficit. Coppell's men could have wrapped up the game when the fifth penalty was awarded, but John Pemberton blasted the ball over the bar. Perry Suckling had to make an FAntastic save near the end to ensure that Palace took maximum points and the majority of the 14,384 crowd went home happy.

TUESDAY 28TH MARCH 1950

Chairman David Harris and the new Crystal Palace owners handed manager Ronnie Rooke £20,000 to strengthen the playing staff. It was a decision that the inexperienced board would later come to regret as Rooke immediately purchased a number of highly-paid veterans, obliterating the club transfer fee record in the process no less than three times, culminating with the purchase of Bill Whittaker from Huddersfield Town for £10,000.

SATURDAY 28TH MARCH 1987

Mark Bright ensured local bragging rights went to Palace as he scored the only goal in a 1-0 win over Millwall.

SATURDAY 28TH MARCH 1998

Chris Armstrong scored on his return to Selhurst Park, as his new side Tottenham Hotspur triumphed 3-1 in a relegation six-pointer. Crystal Palace were bottom of the Premiership and had needed to beat fellow strugglers Spurs to get within two points of the North Londoners.

SATURDAY 28TH MARCH 1999

Steve Coppell lost five of his first-team players ahead of the fixture against high-flying Bradford City, as chairman Mark Goldberg made drastic attempts to cut the wage bill. But Coppell rallied his men and Fan Zhiyi was the man on target as Palace beat Bradford City 1-0 at Selhurst Park, which extended the Eagles' unbeaten run to seven matches in the most adverse of circumstances. Sasa Curcic, who wasn't playing, wandered the touchline with a placard that stated "Stop NATO bombing" as his home country of Serbia took a pounding from the war planes.

TUESDAY 29TH MARCH 2005

Crystal Palace defender Tony Popovic came on as a substitute for former Eagle Craig Moore in Australia's 3-0 friendly win against Indonesia. Proceeds from the game went to victims of the December tsunami.

FRIDAY 30TH MARCH 1973

With Crystal Palace struggling in the top flight, the board of directors moved Bert Head "upstairs" and gave him the title of "General Manager" whilst appointing Malcolm Allison as team manager. At 6pm a young Jim Cannon was the first player to meet the new manager and was immediately told he would be selected for his first ever Palace squad for the next day's fixture against Chelsea.

WEDNESDAY 30TH MARCH 1983

Steve Coppell played his last game for England, a European Championship qualifier against Greece in front of 44,051 at Wembley that finished 0-0. Also present in the starting XI that day were Kenny Sansom and Trevor Francis. In just over 14 months' time Coppell would become manager of Crystal Palace

SATURDAY 30TH MARCH 1996

Crystal Palace hammered Millwall 4-1 at The New Den with Nigel Martyn also saving a penalty. On loan from West Ham, full-back Kenny Brown scored on his debut to help the Eagles to a crucial three points in the race to get out of the First Division and back into the Premiership.

SATURDAY 31ST MARCH 1973

Ahead of the home fixture against Chelsea, Malcolm Allison strode to the centre circle flanked by general manager Bert Head and chairman Ray Bloye to be hailed by the Selhurst Park faithful. The 19-year-old defender Jim Cannon was handed his first league start and headed home Crystal Palace's second goal from a Don Rogers cross just before the hour to seal a crucial 2-0 win. In 32 games over four seasons against London opposition in the top flight, this was Palace's first win.

FRIDAY 31ST MARCH 1961

The record Fourth Division crowd of 37,774 turned up for the Good Friday derby fixture against Millwall. Unfortunately, the Lions won 2-0.

MONDAY 31ST MARCH 1975

Two brothers lined up for opposite sides as Alan Whittle turned out for Crystal Palace while Graham appeared for Wrexham at the Racecourse Ground.

CRYSTAL PALACE
On This Day

APRIL

SATURDAY 1st APRIL 1961

Johnny Byrne scored his 29th and 30th league goals of the season in a 2-1 home win over Oldham Athletic. Byrne didn't notch again that campaign, but his tally of thirty league strikes was a post-war record that still stands as at August 2008.

MONDAY 1st APRIL 2002

Steve Bruce's much hyped return to Selhurst Park after his resignation as manager failed to deliver fireworks on the pitch as Crystal Palace and Birmingham played out a dull and dour 0-0 draw in Division One. The Eagles' best efforts were from Danny Granville's free-kicks that peppered Nico Vaesen's goal. In the lead-up to the game, Bruce had issued an apology, of sorts, to the Palace fans when he admitted he had let them down "big style" when quitting South London but insisted he "had his reasons".

SATURDAY 2nd APRIL 2005

Ahead of the crucial Premiership home game with Middlesbrough, manager Iain Dowie had called on the fans to turn Selhurst Park into a fortress. But, whatever the atmosphere down in SE25, Steve McClaren's men took all three points from their raid and plunged the Eagles further into relegation trouble courtesy of French defender Franck Queudrue who headed the only goal of the game.

SATURDAY 3rd APRIL 1976

Crystal Palace failed to do themselves justice and lost a dour FA Cup semi-final against Second Division Southampton 2-0 at Stamford Bridge.

THURSDAY 3rd APRIL 1986

The 'Palace Lifeline' was launched at Fairfield Halls with the sole intention of fans raising funds for Steve Coppell to buy players with. Anton Otulakowski was the first player to be purchased with the money raised.

MONDAY 3rd APRIL 1995

Work started on the roof of the new Holmesdale Road stand as the construction began to take shape at Selhurst Park. The roof sections had already been made in Fleetwood, Lancashire, and were transported down to SE25 on the back of low-loader trucks.

SATURDAY 3RD APRIL 1999

Emotional scenes at Carrow Road as Steve Coppell led his battered Crystal Palace side to a 1-0 win over Norwich City thanks to Dean Austin's first goal in seven years. With the club in administration, Coppell's men had to drive up from South London to East Anglia and only arrived at the ground 45 minutes before kick-off. With senior players having been shipped out in an attempt to cut the crippling wage bill, four 19-year-olds were in the starting line-up and Coppell also chose to leave out Serbian stars Sasa Curcic and Gordan Petric on compassionate grounds after further NATO bombing strikes on their home city of Belgrade. "Their situation with families back home in Belgrade puts everything else into perspective. Sasa's father was standing on his balcony watching the bombs land and apparently he got a back-draught which pushed him into his flat," stated the Palace boss. On top of all that, a number of players weren't getting paid and were due to meet the next day to discuss strike action. For the 2,000 travelling fans this result in the face of adversity proved the club wouldn't die.

TUESDAY 3RD APRIL 2001

Crystal Palace were held to a 0-0 draw by Huddersfield Town in a crucial relegation battle in Division One as both teams fought for their league lives. The Eagles had pressed through Clinton Morrison and Mikael Forssell in the second half, but it was defender Matthew Upson, on loan from Arsenal, who had the best chance to put Palace ahead but he could only head into the grateful arms of Terriers goalkeeper Nico Vaesen, from five yards out.

FRIDAY 4TH APRIL 1969

A bumper Good Friday crowd of 41,381 was present at Selhurst Park for the crucial clash between Crystal Palace and Middlesbrough. With 0-0 the result, the Glaziers remained in second spot courtesy of a superior goal average.

SATURDAY 4TH APRIL 1964

Crystal Palace nicked a point away at high-flying Hull thanks to a contentious penalty that Cliff Holton coolly put away. A local was so incensed that he ran onto the pitch and struck 5ft 6ins Palace midfielder Bobby Kellard. Although the police caught the culprit, Kellard refused to press charges and instead the assailant was marched to the dressing room to apologise to a highly amused Palace team.

SATURDAY 4TH APRIL 1981

Dario Gradi took Crystal Palace back into the second tier of English football as his team were relegated with just under a month of the season to go, following a 1-0 defeat by Manchester United.

SATURDAY 5TH APRIL 1980

Crystal Palace and Brighton & Hove Albion met for the first time in the top flight at Selhurst Park. Peter Ward put the Seagulls in front, but Jim Cannon rescued the day for the majority of the 31,466 crowd when his equaliser salvaged a point.

MONDAY 5TH APRIL 1999

With threatened strike action due to unpaid wages called off, the players of Crystal Palace gave their all as Sunderland, on their way to the title with a record 105 points, visited Selhurst Park. Clinton Morrison cancelled out Kevin Phillips' opener to earn a deserved point.

MONDAY 6TH APRIL 1970

Crystal Palace ended their first-ever top-flight campaign by beating Manchester City 1-0 at Selhurst Park, thus completing the league double having won at Maine Road in March. Despite it being Palace's last game, they were not yet assured of their First Division status as either Sunderland or Sheffield Wednesday could gain three points from their remaining two fixtures and catch them.

SATURDAY 6TH APRIL 1940

Crystal Palace recorded their biggest ever competitive victory when they hammered Brighton 10-0 in the wartime Football League South 'D' Division. Palace won the league, four points clear of QPR, and scored 64 goals in the 18 matches.

MONDAY 6TH APRIL 1931

Peter Simpson bagged the last of his seven league hat-tricks for the season in a pulsating 4-4 draw away at Swindon. Simpson would end the campaign with 46 league strikes to his name, having started all 42 games. Simpson's tally still stands as a record and is unlikely to ever be beaten. Ironically, Swindon were the team that Palace had scored most of their hat-tricks against: six in total.

SUNDAY 7TH APRIL 1991

Crystal Palace returned to Wembley less than a year after losing the FA Cup final to finally win some silverware at the famous stadium, in the form of the Full Members Cup, beating Everton 4-1 after extra time in front of 40,000 delirious Palace fans who made up the majority of the 52,460 attendance. Ian Wright plundered two of the goals with John Salako and Geoff Thomas also notching. But in the words of the chant, as "Geoff goes up to lift the Zenith cup", Toffees keeper Neville Southall refused to walk up the stairs to collect his runners-up medal, deciding to stage a one-man protest by sitting and sulking at his goal-post. The competition was the brainchild of Ron Noades and Chelsea chairman Ken Bates.

SATURDAY 7TH APRIL 2001

Tommy Black plundered a dramatic 88th minute goal to give Crystal Palace a 2-2 draw at Vicarage Road against play-off chasing Watford. Dean Austin had put the Eagles ahead in the 14th minute from the penalty spot after Ricardo Fuller had been up-ended by Hornets skipper Robert Page, but Watford equalised in the 76th minute through Allan Nielsen. Tommy Mooney added a second moments later when he lashed a 25-yard effort past Kolinko.

TUESDAY 8TH APRIL 1986

Andy Gray nabbed a brace as Crystal Palace beat Portsmouth 2-1 at Selhurst Park in front of 11,731. The goals were Gray's last for the season, and he ended the campaign top scorer with ten.

SUNDAY 8TH APRIL 1990

Most pundits had written off Crystal Palace's chances against Liverpool in the FA Cup semi-final before they had even kicked-off at Villa Park. The Eagles were without the injured Ian Wright and Eddie McGoldrick, as well as having lost 9-0 at Anfield earlier in the season. Inevitably, Steve McMahon put the Merseysiders 1-0 up after just 14 minutes, having sprung Palace's offside trap. The goal celebrations of the Liverpool players were muted as they believed they were on their way to a routine victory. At the interval, Coppell told his players not to worry, saying anything could happen. How right he was! Straight from the restart, John Pemberton bombed down the right flank before putting over a cross that, after a spot of pinball in the area, Mark Bright lashed home. Palace were back on level terms and had cracked Liverpool's shield of invincibility. The Eagles dominated from here on in, going ahead in the 69th minute thanks to Gary O'Reilly's close range effort following an Andy Gray free-kick. Dalglish's men dug deep and levelled the game at 2-2 thanks to a McMahon drive, and then went ahead in the 83rd minute when John Barnes scored from the penalty spot following referee George Courtney's harsh adjudgement that Pemberton had fouled Steve Staunton. At 3-2 down and going out of the cup, Andy Gray was the hero as he nodded home to level two minutes from time. Andy Thorn might have won it moments later had his powerful header not smashed against the crossbar. In to extra time... In the 109th minute of the match, Palace sealed an FAmous 4-3 victory when Alan Pardew headed the winner after Gray's corner was flicked on by Thorn. The cup holders were out and Crystal Palace were going to Wembley for their first FA Cup final appearance.

MONDAY 9TH APRIL 1951

Away at Port Vale in the league, Crystal Palace were getting hammered 5-1 on a pitch that was nothing short of a mud-bath. With an hour of the game gone the referee abandoned the match, much to the visitors' relief. The replayed game later in the month saw Palace sneak a 2-2 draw!

FRIDAY 9TH APRIL 1993

Crystal Palace went down 4-0 in the rain to Wimbledon in the away leg of the Landlord versus Tenant derby. It left Steve Coppell's men with a relegation battle on their hands.

SUNDAY 9TH APRIL 1995

Crystal Palace faced Manchester United at Villa Park in the semi-final of the FA Cup in a pulsating contest witnessed by 38,256 fans. Iain Dowie headed the Eagles in front, before United levelled. Chris Armstrong lobbed Peter Schmeichel from 15 yards to take it to 2-1 in extra time before Gary Pallister saved the day for Alex Ferguson by netting the equaliser to force a replay. The whole day was soured by news that a Crystal Palace season ticket holder, Paul Nixon, had been killed after the group he was in had been attacked by Manchester United fans outside a pub in Walsall. Nixon ultimately died when he fell under the coach he had been travelling on and was crushed, having been assaulted. Tensions between Palace and Manchester United fans had been heightened after the Eric Cantona incident in January.

MONDAY 10TH APRIL 1995

Nigel Martyn realised he had a broken finger after the FA Cup semi-final the day before. The index finger of his left hand suffered in a collision with David Beckham in the second minute of the game. The big Cornishman was out of the replay and the crucial relegation run-in.

SATURDAY 11TH APRIL 1998

In the programme for the Premiership game with Leicester City, Ron Noades reflected on the fact that the Eagles constantly being linked with the likes of Paul Gascoigne, Ally McCoist, John Barnes and Andy Goram had been unsettling the staff and players. Noades also pointed out that the recommendation for Attilio Lombardo's recent appointment as manager had come from Steve Coppell himself. The game itself saw Lombardo's men lose 3-0 to Martin O'Neill's mob, Emile Heskey bagging a brace before Matt Elliot added the third. Midfielder Patricio Billio, on-loan from AC Milan, made his only start for Crystal Palace having been a substitute in two previous games. It was to be the Italian's last time in a Palace shirt before moving to Dundee, and his three appearances for the Eagles put him in such exalted company as: Argentinian and former Boca Juniors midfielder Walter Del Rio, who ironically moved to Dundee after making one start and two substitute appearances in the 1998/99 season; forward Nicola Ventola, who made three substitute appearances in the 2004/05 Premiership season after moving to Selhurst Park on a season-long loan from Inter Milan; Slovenian defender Amir Karic, on loan from Ipswich Town, who made three starts in March 2001 and former West Ham defender Tony Gale.

SATURDAY 12TH APRIL 1980

Crystal Palace beat Leeds United 1-0 at Selhurst Park, but it was their only victory in the last ten games of the season. This dip in form saw the Eagles collapse to finish 13th in the First Division, sowing the seeds for what would be the disastrous 1980/81 relegation campaign.

TUESDAY 12TH APRIL 1995

The FA refused to postpone the replay of the FA Cup semi-final against Manchester United in light of the tragic death of Crystal Palace supporter Paul Nixon, so a large number of Palace fans boycotted the replay as their own personal mark of respect, and at the request of director Colin Noades. Some Eagles fans travelled and they contributed to an attendance of just 17,987 at Villa Park. The crowd was addressed by Alan Smith and Alex Ferguson before the game, followed by a well-observed minute's silence. Pre-match pleas for calm were heeded by both sets of supporters, but the message didn't get through to Roy Keane. With his team 2-0 up and cruising, Keane was fairly slide-tackled by Gareth Southgate, but was inadvertently caught on his injured ankle. The Irishman reacted furiously, got up and stamped on Southgate's stomach as he laid prone following the challenge. It earned Keane his first red card in the English game. In the inevitable melee that followed, Darren Patterson was singled out by the referee for an early bath as he evened things up on the pitch. "It wasn't a personal thing," Keane would later recall. "One of his teammates had been winding me up and he was just in the wrong place at the wrong time." Palace eventually lost 2-0, leaving them free to concentrate on staying in the Premiership.

SATURDAY 13TH APRIL 2002

Tickets went on sale for Simon Rodger's testimonial match against Tottenham Hotspur.

THURSDAY 14TH APRIL 1966

Bury gaffer Bert Head took over as manager of Crystal Palace following a series of meetings with chairman Arthur Wait. Summing up the appointment, the Shakers chairman proclaimed "We've lost, and you've got, the best manager in the business."

SIMON RODGER

FRIDAY 14TH APRIL 1995

Crystal Palace went 1-0 up against Tottenham Hotspur in a Premiership game at Selhurst thanks to Chris Armstrong. But, Jurgen Klinsmann dispatched a spectacular free-kick in the 88th minute to earn Spurs a point and plunged Alan Smith's men deeper into the mire.

WEDNESDAY 15TH APRIL 1970

Third from bottom Crystal Palace, league fixtures completed, looked on as Sunderland were relegated from the First Division when they lost their last game of the season 1-0 at home to Liverpool. With two going down only Sheffield Wednesday, who grabbed a point with a 2-2 draw away at Manchester United, could overhaul Palace.

FRIDAY 15TH APRIL 1960

Crystal Palace beat Exeter City 1-0 at Selhurst Park in the first of three league games over four days during Easter. The result left the Glaziers with an outside chance of sneaking into the fourth spot and with it the last remaining promotion space on offer. Manager George Smith had vowed to leave at the end of the season if he didn't get his men into the Third Division, so plans were put into place to move assistant Arthur Rowe into the hot seat.

FRIDAY 16TH APRIL 1954

One of the last amateurs to play for Crystal Palace, centre-forward Keith Morton, made his debut in the 2-0 defeat away at Ipswich Town. Morton played the last four matches of the season, notching three times.

TUESDAY 16TH APRIL 1974

Fulham defeated Crystal Palace 2-0 at Selhurst Park which sent the Eagles third from bottom. With typical Palace timing, this was the first season that "three up and three down" was introduced...

SATURDAY 16TH APRIL 1988

Crystal Palace made their first ever appearance at Wembley in the Mercantile Credit Tournament, staged to celebrate the centenary of the Football League. In the multi-team tournament the Eagles faced Sheffield Wednesday at 5.30pm. After twenty minutes each way of goalless action, penalties were used to settle the tie which Yorkshire team won 2-1.

TUESDAY 17TH APRIL 1979

Over 30,000 packed into Selhurst on Easter Tuesday to see Jerry Murphy covert a Steve Kember cross to give Crystal Palace a 1-0 victory over local rivals Charlton. The result kept the Eagles in third spot, a point behind Stoke and Brighton but with a game in hand.

WEDNESDAY 18TH APRIL 1962

The absolute undisputed kings of European football, Real Madrid, headed to SE25 for a prestigious friendly to mark the new £18,000, 100ft floodlights at Selhurst Park. The Spanish wanted £10,000 to play, so Third Division Crystal Palace put their prices up for the fixture and actually made a £5,000 profit on the venture as 24,740 turned up on a cold night to see Di Stefano and Puskas mix it with Terry Long and Roy Summersby, as well as Johnny Byrne who West Ham United had allowed to come back and guest for Palace. The five times European Cup holders, who would go on to win the famous trophy again in 1966, ran out 4-3 winners.

SATURDAY 18TH APRIL 1998

Crystal Palace got their first home Premiership win of the season, nine months into the league campaign when they defeated Derby County 3-1 in front of 18,101. It was player-manager Lombardo's first win in four games but the three points still left the Eagles rock bottom of the Premiership.

FRIDAY 18TH APRIL 2003

Simon Jordan ordered a summer clear-out of players, rounding on the "big-time Charlies" who failed to deliver. But Trevor Francis wasn't going to be the man doing it, as he left the club by "mutual consent". Once again, Steve Kember stepped into the breach and was appointed caretaker manager.

SATURDAY 19TH APRIL 1969

Crystal Palace entered the penultimate game of the season in second place, with only Charlton statistically capable of hauling their South London neighbours back. Before the match, the Palace Dolly Girls lined up in front of the Main Stand at Selhurst Park to receive orchids from the players. The 36,126 fans then witnessed Palace go 2-0 down against Fulham, only for Steve Kember and Mark Lazarus to drag the Glaziers back into it. Cliff Jackson then sealed the win, and with the Addicks losing anyway, Palace were promoted to the top flight for the very first time in their history.

WEDNESDAY 19TH APRIL 1961

Crystal Palace secured a promotion 40 years after their last one when they beat Aldershot 2-1 at Selhurst Park in front of nearly 20,000 to go up to the Third Division. The Hampshire side ran Palace close, taking the lead after 15 minutes before Roy Summersby equalised after 35 minutes. Tom Barnett sealed maximum points for the Glaziers when he headed home George Petchey's cross three minutes from time.

SUNDAY 20TH APRIL 1969

The *Sunday Mirror* declared the 36,126 who roared Crystal Palace on to promotion to the First Division in the 3-2 win over Fulham at Selhurst Park, the "Crowd of the Season" in their "Crowd Awards."

FRIDAY 20TH APRIL 1978

Crystal Palace travelled to Leicester for a rare Friday night fixture. A crucial point was salvaged through a Paul Hinshelwood equaliser.

THURSDAY 20TH APRIL 1995

Crystal Palace travelled to Ewood Park for a league fixture and ended up losing 2-1 to the Premiership champions-elect, Blackburn Rovers. Relegation was now a distinct possibility.

FRIDAY 20TH APRIL 2007

Crystal Palace USA, officially known as 'Crystal Palace Baltimore', played their first-ever competitive match, against the Charlotte Eagles in the United Soccer League Division Two. Taking place at Waddell High School, Crystal Palace lost 4-1, although big Malian-born defender Ibrahim Kante did score Palace USA's first-ever competitive goal.

SUNDAY 21ST APRIL 2002

Channel 4 documentary *The Players*, a series based on the Crystal Palace academy, aired for the first time. Cameras followed club scholars as they attempted to make their way in the game with the first episode featuring Wayne Routledge and Craig Dobson discussing their dreams of becoming professional footballers.

SUNDAY 21st APRIL 2002

Crystal Palace lost 2-0 against West Bromwich Albion at the Hawthorns, which saw the Baggies return to the Premier League and Palace finish their First Division campaign a disappointing tenth. Manager Trevor Francis stated: "I know some of the supporters will be disappointed where we have finished but it must be remembered that a mid-table position is a great credit to everyone at the club."

WEDNESDAY 22nd APRIL 1970

Sheffield Wednesday faced mid-table Manchester City in their last game of the season needing a handsome win in order to finish third from bottom and so escape relegation, condemning Crystal Palace to the second tier in the process. But, City triumphed 2-1 at Hillsborough to leave Bert Head's men safe, over two weeks after Palace's own league campaign had actually ended.

WEDNESDAY 22nd APRIL 1964

Crystal Palace drew 2-2 away to relegation-bound Wrexham in the penultimate game of the season to secure promotion to the Second Division. It had been 39 years since second tier league football had been seen at Selhurst Park.

WEDNESDAY 22nd APRIL 1959

Vic Rouse became the first-ever player from the Fourth Division to gain full international honours when he was chosen to start for Wales in their Home International Championship match against Northern Ireland in Belfast. The Crystal Palace keeper performed credibly but couldn't stop the Welsh from losing 4-1.

WEDNESDAY 22nd APRIL 1981

A season to forget was made even worse off the pitch when a team of Customs and Excise officials moved in to investigate the books at Selhurst Park.

SATURDAY 22nd APRIL 1989

The away fixture against Plymouth Argyle at Home Park kicked off at 3.06pm after a minute's silence had been observed in memory of those who died in the tragedy at Hillsborough the previous Saturday.

SUNDAY 23rd APRIL 2006

Crystal Palace announced that they had launched an "Academy and Developmental Club" in the USA, with the intention to have a system for identifying and developing the best young talent in the United States. Palace Director of Football Bob Dowie boldly enthused that everyone at the club "wanted to develop the footprint of Crystal Palace worldwide".

SATURDAY 24th APRIL 1965

Crystal Palace lost 3-2 away to Ipswich Town in the last game of the season but still managed to finish seventh in their first season back in the Second Division for 39 years.

TUESDAY 24th APRIL 1973

Away to fellow relegation strugglers Norwich City, Crystal Palace needed a win in their last away game of the season to stand any chance of beating the drop. But the Canaries made themselves safe when they scored deep into second-half injury time to win the match 2-1, a result which condemned Malcolm Allison's men to the second tier.

SATURDAY 25th APRIL 1964

Needing just a point to return as champions to the Second Division, Crystal Palace messed it up in front of their biggest crowd for nearly three seasons when they crashed 3-1 to Oldham. The defeat, in front of 28,000 at Selhurst, handed the title to Coventry City who won 1-0 at home to Colchester United. The Glaziers made do with promotion via the runners-up spot alongside news that Millwall had been relegated to the Fourth Division.

SATURDAY 25th APRIL 1987

Mark Bright and Ian Wright did the business as Crystal Palace beat Oldham Athletic 2-0 at Boundary Park in the first of many games in which they were the only two scorers.

TUESDAY 25th APRIL 1989

Crystal Palace finally played their away fixture against Swindon Town, which had been postponed since the opening day of the season. But Coppell's men should not have bothered, as Lou Macari's promotion-chasing side won 1-0.

SATURDAY 25TH APRIL 1992

Mark Bright scored his 17th and last league goal of the season in the 1-1 draw at Sheffield Wednesday. His haul was the second highest tally for a Palace player in the top flight, Andrew Johnson having scored 21 in 2004/05.

SATURDAY 26TH APRIL 1958

Crystal Palace crashed 4-1 at home to Southampton in the last league game of the season. A 14th place finish meant a de facto relegation as teams in the bottom half of Division Three (South), together with their counterparts from the northern competition, had to start the 1958/59 season in the newly formed Fourth Division.

SATURDAY 26TH APRIL 1980

Dave Swindlehurst made his loan move to Derby County permanent after the Rams broke their record transfer fee when they shelled out £400,000 for the Edgeware-born forward. But, on the day Swindlehurst formally signed, Derby were relegated from the top flight despite beating Manchester City 3-1 at the Baseball Ground.

SATURDAY 26TH APRIL 1986

Ian Wright scored his 8th and 9th goals of the season as Crystal Palace dismissed Barnsley 4-2 in front of just 3,862 at Oakwell.

SATURDAY 26TH APRIL 1997

Two goals from Neil Shipperley helped Crystal Palace to a 2-0 win over Swindon Town in their last away game of the season. The three points collected guaranteed the Eagles a place in the play-offs.

MONDAY 27TH APRIL 1959

Crystal Palace lost 2-1 to Arsenal in the final of the Southern Floodlit Cup at Selhurst Park. A 32,384 crowd generated record gate receipts of £3,700. Johnny Byrne hit an equaliser with ten minutes to go only for Mel Charles, brother of Welsh legend John Charles, to win it for the North Londoners.

SATURDAY 27TH APRIL 1974

A huge away following travelled down to the County Ground to see Crystal Palace beat Swindon Town 1-0 in the penultimate game of the season, which kept the battle to avoid relegation alive.

MONDAY 27TH APRIL 1998

Crystal Palace were finally relegated from the Premiership as Manchester United beat them 3-0 in a Sky game at Selhurst Park in front of 26,180. The Eagles had also had an FArcical season off the pitch due to the protracted takeover from Ron Noades by Mark Goldberg.

MONDAY 28TH APRIL 1969

Crystal Palace took to the field at Ewood Park in the last game of the season to gracious applause from the Blackburn players, for the Glaziers had secured promotion to the First Division as runners-up to Brian Clough's Derby, who had already won the title. Palace won the game 2-1, but the late sending off of John McCormick and Rovers' Frank Kopel soured the night.

WEDNESDAY 28TH APRIL 1954

After a 1-1 home draw with runners-up Brighton & Hove Albion, Palace ended the season third from bottom in Division Three (South).

SATURDAY 28TH APRIL 1923

Palace finished a credible 16th in only their second season in the Football League's Second Division. The last home game of the campaign saw hapless Wolves demolished 5-0.

SUNDAY 28TH APRIL 1996

Palace took on Derby County in the penultimate league game of the season at the Baseball Ground. The winners were guaranteed second spot and automatic promotion to the Premiership. Rams boss Jim Smith bombastically called the fixture "bigger than the World Cup final". Derby went 1-0 up within minutes, then Kenny Brown equalised moments later. But Rams skipper Robin van der Laan broke Palace hearts when he leapt unchallenged to head the winner in the second half. The Eagles made do with a third place finish and the play-offs.

SATURDAY 28TH APRIL 2001

Palace were left on the brink of relegation to English football's third tier after they capitulated in the last home game of the season, losing 2-0 to ten-man Wolves. The 18,993 crowd demanded manager Alan Smith's head and called for the reinstatement of Steve Coppell. The only hope of avoiding the drop rested on final day results elsewhere going their way.

SATURDAY 29TH APRIL 1961

Roy Summersby scored his 25th, and Palace's 110th, league goal of the season in their 1-0 victory over York City in the final fixture of the campaign. The points ensured the Glaziers finished in the runner's-up spot to earn promotion to the Third Division, whilst the tally of goals scored by the team for the season set a new record that still stands.

SATURDAY 29TH APRIL 1972

Palace drew 0-0 with Huddersfield Town at Selhurst Park on the last day of the season. A fourth successive season in the top flight beckoned as the Glaziers finished 20th, four points clear of the drop zone.

SATURDAY 29TH APRIL 1978

Crystal Palace recorded their biggest victory of the Second Division campaign when they hammered Blackburn Rovers 5-0 at Selhurst Park.

WEDNESDAY 29TH APRIL 1998

Attilio Lombardo was fired and chairman Ron Noades stepped into the gaffer's role, assisted by Ray Lewington and Brian Sparrow.

SATURDAY 29TH APRIL 2000

Crystal Palace secured their Division One status in the last home game of the season thanks to a 2-1 win over Blackburn Rovers. Ashley Cole and Clinton Morrison were on target for the Eagles.

SUNDAY 29TH APRIL 2001

After a 2-0 loss to Wolves left Palace on the brink of relegation to Division Two, Simon Jordan sacked manager Alan Smith and coach Ray Houghton. Long-standing Palace hero Steve Kember was given mission impossible; keep the Eagles up.

MONDAY 30TH APRIL 1956

Two days after the regular end of the season, Crystal Palace faced Shrewsbury Town at Gay Meadow needing at least a win to stand any chance of finishing outside the bottom two and having to again apply for re-election. But the Glaziers lost 2-0, and finished the campaign on 34 points. Millwall rubbed salt into the wounds by winning their last league game to finish third from bottom with 36 points.

SATURDAY 30TH APRIL 1921

Crystal Palace were inaugural champions of the Football League's Third Division after they came from 1-0 down and claimed a point with a 2-2 draw away at Northampton. Club chairman Sydney Bourne congratulated manager Edmund Goodman and his team for the "happy conclusion of a strenuous fight". The result was also relayed back to a joyous crowd at The Nest, who had turned up to see Palace reserves take on Gillingham's second string.

TUESDAY 30TH APRIL 1974

Crystal Palace had to beat Cardiff City at Ninian Park to avoid a second successive relegation and Third Division football. Cardiff needed just a draw to stay in the Second Division. The 5,000 Palace fans in the 26,781 crowd went crazy when Stewart Jump converted Peter Taylor's corner to put the Eagles in the lead in the 29th minute, but joy turned to despair when Cardiff equalised five minutes later. The game finished 1-1 and Palace were relegated to the third tier of English football along with Preston and Swindon.

CRYSTAL PALACE
On This Day

MAY

WEDNESDAY 1st MAY 1957

The final game of the season saw Torquay United visit Selhurst Park, with the Devon side needing a win to gain promotion to the Second Division. The Glaziers spoiled the party by getting a 1-1 draw, a result that saw Ipswich Town, under Alf Ramsey, finish top courtesy of goal average. Crystal Palace themselves finished a lowly 20th.

SATURDAY 1st MAY 1993

Crystal Palace beat Ipswich Town 3-1 in their last home game of the season to go eight points ahead of Oldham Athletic, who occupied the final relegation berth in 20th place. The Eagles had two games left to play, the Latics had three including tough fixtures against Aston Villa and Liverpool. Steve Coppell sent his players on a lap-of-honour around Selhurst Park, as everyone had thought they had done enough to beat the drop...

SUNDAY 1st MAY 1994

Crystal Palace beat Middlesbrough 3-2 at Ayresome Park in front of the ITV cameras to clinch the Football League Division One title, ensuring the Eagles returned to the top flight as champions.

SATURDAY 1st MAY 1999

Crystal Palace's last home game of the administration season saw the Grim Reaper march on Selhurst Park as the fans called for Mark Goldberg's resignation in order to save the club. The match itself saw Steve Coppell's teenagers grab a 2-2 draw on their way to mid-table finish in Division One.

SATURDAY 1st MAY 2004

Tommy Black came on as an 83th minute substitute and five minutes later he was falling over Walsall defender Paul Ritchie in the box. Andy Johnson scored the disputed penalty, and Crystal Palace won 1-0, taking them into the play-off spots.

SATURDAY 2nd MAY 1931

Palace demolished Torquay 5-0 at home on the last day of the season to clinch the runners-up spot in the Football League Third Division (South). Notts County had been the pacesetters all season and finished the season as champions, eight points clear of Palace.

SATURDAY 2ND MAY 1925

In the last game of the Second Division season, Crystal Palace faced Oldham Athletic at Selhurst Park in a fixture they had to win to avoid relegation. The tension was palpable amongst the assembled 20,000 but with just 15 minutes left and with the score at 0-0, Oldham took the lead when Billy Callender, in goal for his first senior appearance of the season, was beaten. It was the only goal of the game and Palace, along with Coventry City, were relegated to the Third Division (South). It was 39 years before Second Division football returned to Selhurst Park.

SATURDAY 2ND MAY 1981

Crystal Palace bowed out of the First Division with a 1-1 draw away to Manchester City. The final table didn't make for pleasant reading as the Eagles ended the season rock-bottom on just 19 points, a full 13 points behind Leicester City, the club immediately above them.

SUNDAY 2ND MAY 1993

In the battle to avoid relegation from the Premier League, Oldham unexpectedly beat Aston Villa away to move within five points of Crystal Palace with two games left of the season.

WEDNESDAY 2ND MAY 2001

An emotion-charged night down on the south coast as a capacity crowd of 19,013 squeezed into Fratton Park to see a Dougie Freedman-inspired Palace put four past Portsmouth, which lifted the Eagles out of the bottom three of Division One and at the same time sent the Hampshire club into the relegation spots for the first time that season. Caretaker-manager Steve Kember had remodelled the starting XI and it had paid the most handsome of dividends. Suddenly, it looked like the great escape could be on.

SATURDAY 3RD MAY 1952

Crystal Palace ended the season in 19th spot after a 3-3 draw against Northampton Town at Selhurst Park. Ironically, manager Laurie Scott had joined when the Glaziers were in 19th earlier in the season.

TUESDAY 3RD MAY 1977

Crystal Palace kept their promotion hopes alive with a crucial 2-1 win over high-flying Wrexham at Selhurst Park in a tense Division Three clash.

SATURDAY 3rd MAY 1924

The last ever game at The Nest saw Palace beat Barnsley 3-1 in a Second Division fixture. The 1924/25 season would see the club installed at nearby Selhurst Park.

THURSDAY 3rd MAY 1973

Bert Head quietly resigned the position of general manager having led Crystal Palace to the top flight for the first time in their history, and then kept them there for three consecutive seasons.

TUESDAY 4th MAY 1971

Palace were hammered 6-0 by Saints at The Dell on the final day of the season but still ended up with a credible 18th place finish in only their second season in the top flight.

WEDNESDAY 4th MAY 1960

The season ended with a 0-0 draw away at Gillingham. The point saw the Glaziers languishing in 8th spot, a position that led to the departure of manager George Smith after he promised to leave if he didn't get the Selhurst Park outfit promoted.

WEDNESDAY 4th MAY 1955

Crystal Palace beat Norwich City 2-0 at Selhurst Park in the final match of the season to ensure they finished in 20th spot and didn't have to seek another re-election.

SATURDAY 4th MAY 1929

Palace went into the final game of the season level on points with Charlton Athletic at the top of the league, but the Addicks boasted the better goal average. There were 22,000 fans present at Selhurst Park to watch Palace beat a spirited Brighton & Hove Albion side 1-0, the goal coming late on via a 70th minute penalty from skipper Stan Charlton. But it was not enough to secure the title, as Charlton sealed a 2-0 win away at Walsall to condemn Palace to the runners-up spot and another season in the Third Division (South).

SATURDAY 4TH MAY 1991

A hat-trick from Ian Wright plundered in just 18 frantic minutes of second-half football inspired Crystal Palace to a 3-0 win over Wimbledon in the final ever league game at Plough Lane, in front of 10,002. It was Palace's first hat-trick at an away ground since 1963 and their fastest in the top flight. Wright's second goal, a 40-yard lob over Hans Segers, was described by Steve Coppell as "one of the finest pieces of individual skill I have ever seen". The Dons had to leave their ground of 79 years due to the Taylor Report, and headed for Selhurst Park to replace Charlton Athletic. The Addicks were meant to go back to the Valley, but had to share West Ham's Upton Park ground when work had not been completed on time.

MONDAY 4TH MAY 1998

Crystal Palace lost 2-1 away at Gillingham in the last game of the season to finish 14th in the Championship, Dougie Freedman scoring a consolation penalty.

SATURDAY 5TH MAY 1951

Having not won away since March, it's no surprise that Crystal Palace ended the season with a 3-1 defeat to Norwich at Carrow Road. It capped another miserable season for the Glaziers as they again finished bottom of the Third Division (South) on 27 points, two points adrift of Watford. For the second time in three seasons, Palace had to apply for re-election to the Football League.

SATURDAY 5TH MAY 1979

The final weekend in the 1978/79 Division 2 campaign saw Crystal Palace vying for one of three promotion spots alongside Brighton & Hove Albion, Stoke City and Sunderland. All four sides had won away from home, with the Eagles recording a 1-0 win at Leyton Orient. But thanks to a postponed fixture, Terry Venables' men had one last game the following Friday at home to Burnley in which to secure passage to the top flight...

SATURDAY 5TH MAY 1984

Crystal Palace guaranteed their league status in their penultimate home match when they dispatched already relegated Swansea City 2-0 courtesy of Jim Cannon and a fit again Kevin Mabbutt. It was also Peter Nicholas' 150th appearance for the Eagles, having returned from Arsenal earlier in the season.

SATURDAY 5TH MAY 1990

Ahead of the FA Cup final appearance against Manchester United, Crystal Palace faced their city rivals in the last game of the league campaign at Selhurst Park. The Manchester City fans were allowed to parade on the pitch, which was straw yellow due to a combination of prolonged sunshine and herbicide, with banners urging Palace to deny United a victory at Wembley. Palace should have won the game against a lacklustre City, having gone 2-0 up inside ten minutes, but they let Howard Kendall's men grab a draw late on through Niall Quinn, who handled the ball as he strolled through a static Palace defence before prodding past Nigel Martyn. The draw denied Palace a 12th place finish and had to settle for 15th instead. Millwall were relegated from the top flight, having finished bottom.

WEDNESDAY 5TH MAY 1993

In the battle to avoid dropping out of the newly-formed Premier League, Crystal Palace were five points ahead of Oldham Athletic in 20th spot going into the evening's fixtures. At 10pm, following Palace's battling point in a 0-0 draw at Maine Road and Oldham's shock 3-2 victory over Liverpool the difference was now down to three points. If Palace could avoid defeat away to Arsenal in their last game they would be safe...

SATURDAY 6TH MAY 1950

Crystal Palace ended their season limply when they lost 3-1 away at Walsall, but with better goal average they pipped Brighton to a 7th place finish in the league; a distinct improvement on the previous season when they finished bottom and had to apply for re-election to the Football League.

MONDAY 6TH MAY 1985

Trevor Aylott bagged his 8th and final league goal of the season in the 3-0 away win at Cardiff City, ending the campaign as Crystal Palace's top scorer.

SATURDAY 6TH MAY 1995

Crystal Palace beat fellow Premiership strugglers West Ham United 1-0 at a sunny Selhurst Park thanks to Chris Armstrong in what was Gareth Southgate's 150th league game for the Eagles.

SUNDAY 6TH MAY 2001

Palace escaped relegation to the third tier by the narrowest of margins, having headed into the final game of the Division One season out of the bottom three on goal difference but faced with a tricky trip to Edgeley Park to play the already safe Stockport County. A win, with results going their way, was essential to survival. But Kember's men could not find a way past Stockport keeper Lee Jones until late on. As Palace cleared the ball from their area, David Hopkin handled before punting the ball long and hard upfield where it found its way to Dougie Freedman who danced into the opposition box before poking the ball home in the 87th minute for one of the most important goals in the history of Crystal Palace Football Club. But the drama wasn't over, as six minutes of injury time was played, goalkeeper Aleksandrs Kolinko having to back-pedal to make sure a hoofed clearance didn't end up as a sickening equaliser for Stockport. Only Huddersfield Town, who were still playing at home against Birmingham City thanks to a delayed kick-off, could now condemn Palace to the drop. Losing 2-1 to the Blues, Lou Macari's team only needed to snatch a late equaliser to leapfrog Palace on goal difference and save themselves, and they nearly did were it not for the brilliance of Blues keeper Ian Bennett who made a point-blank save late on from Andy Booth. Afterwards, Simon Jordan remarked: "Nothing I have achieved in business means more to me than this."

WEDNESDAY 7TH MAY 1969

Even though England versus Wales was on the TV, and there was torrential rain, over 5,000 Crystal Palace fans turned out to line the route from Selhurst Park to Fairfield Halls where the Mayor of Croydon led a civic reception in honour of Crystal Palace getting promoted to the top flight.

SATURDAY 7TH MAY 1955

Bobby Greener, who made 317 first team appearances between 1921 and 1932, was sacked as Palace's junior team coach.

SATURDAY 7TH MAY 1949

Crystal Palace drew their last game of the season 0-0 away at Port Vale. They finished bottom of the Third Division (South) on 27 points, some six points adrift of Aldershot. Manager Jack Butler was bitterly upset by it all and insisted the club accept his letter of resignation, which they duly did. For the first time, Palace now faced the indignity of having to apply for re-election to the Football League.

SATURDAY 7TH MAY 1932

In their final league fixture, Crystal Palace played out a drab 0-0 with Leyton Orient to ensure they finished the season unbeaten at home. But after two successive runners-up spots, ending the campaign in fourth was seen as a disappointment.

SATURDAY 7TH MAY 1921

Crystal Palace travelled as league champions to Southend United for the last fixture of the Third Division season. Scottish centre-forward John Conner grabbed both goals in a 2-0 win to seal his place as Palace's leading scorer in the league with 29 strikes.

WEDNESDAY 7TH MAY 1975

Kenny Sansom made his debut at 16 years and 223 days old, the third youngest player in Palace's history and the youngest ever to start a game, as the Eagles lost 2-0 away at Tranmere Rovers on the last day of the season.

FRIDAY 7TH MAY 1971

Selhurst Park was the venue for the third/fourth placed play-off in the FA Cup ahead of the final the following day, Stoke City beating Everton 3-2.

SATURDAY 7TH MAY 1988

For the second successive season, Crystal Palace headed into the final game of the season relying on results from other teams in order to land a play-off spot. Steve Coppell's men did their bit by beating Manchester City in front of a season's best crowd of 17,555 at Selhurst Park but our old friends from up the road, Millwall, already crowned Second Division champions, rolled over and succumbed 4-1 at home to Blackburn Rovers when all that was needed was for the Lions to draw. Rovers themselves nicked the last remaining play-off berth.

SATURDAY 8TH MAY 1982

Kevin Mabbutt netted in the 2-1 home defeat by Barnsley, in what was ultimately his last goal of the campaign. His eight league strikes were enough to end the term as Crystal Palace's leading scorer for the season.

SATURDAY 8TH MAY 1993

Crystal Palace lost 3-0 away to Arsenal, and coupled with Oldham beating Southampton at home 4-3, the Eagles slipped through the top-flight trap-door and back into the second-tier of English football. What was particularly frustrating was the amount of points that Palace got relegated on – a massive 49 – and the fact that an old son of ours opened the scoring at Highbury. According to Steve Coppell, it broke Ian Wright's heart to score against his old club in such circumstances.

SUNDAY 8TH MAY 1994

An emotional day at Selhurst Park for the last game of the season, as not only was the 106-year-old Football League trophy presented to Gareth Southgate now that Crystal Palace had wrapped the First Division title up, there was also the small matter of the match marking the last time the Holmesdale Terrace would be in use before it was torn down to be replaced by a two-tier, all seated stand, complete with roof! A capacity 28,749 crowd basked in the sunshine as Watford failed to read the script and won 2-0.

SATURDAY 9TH MAY 1936

Future Crystal Palace manager Jack Butler steered the Belgian national side to an FAmous 3-2 friendly win over England at the Stade du Centenaire in Brussels. It remains Belgium's only ever victory against England.

SATURDAY 9TH MAY 1987

Crystal Palace headed into the final game of the season with an outside chance of making the play-offs if they could beat Hull City at Boothferry Park, and hope that results elsewhere go their way. The dream was dead within a couple of minutes as Alex Dyer opened the scoring and City went on to win 3-0.

SATURDAY 9TH MAY 1995

Palace faced Leeds United in their penultimate game in the league, knowing a win was essential in order to beat the drop out of the Premiership. It was not to be in West Yorkshire, as the Eagles went down 3-1 to leave Alan Smith's men on the brink of a swift return to the second tier of English football.

SUNDAY 9TH MAY 2004

Crystal Palace lost 2-1 to Coventry City in the last game of the season, but still managed to sneak into the play-offs thanks to Brian Deane who scored a last-minute equaliser for West Ham, thus denying Wigan a top-six finish and allowing Iain Dowie's men in.

TUESDAY 9TH MAY 2006

Palace failed to bounce-back at the first attempt to the Premiership when they crashed out of the play-offs at the semi-final stage, losing 3-0 on aggregate to Watford. Although the match at Vicarage Road ended 0-0, the damage had been done in the first leg at Selhurst Park when Palace were beaten 3-0. With action on the pitch at a premium, most will remember the match for the brawl that involved almost every player, back-room staff and both managers that was instigated by Aidy Boothroyd when he prevented Fitz Hall from taking a throw-in.

THURSDAY 10TH MAY 1923

Jack Alderson became the first Crystal Palace goalkeeper to be capped by England when he turned out for them in a tour friendly against France at the Général John Joseph Pershing Stadium, Paris. England went 4-0 up but Alderson failed to keep a clean sheet when he let in an 89th minute consolation for the French. It proved to be Alderson's sole appearance for his country.

THURSDAY 10TH MAY 1979

The *Brighton Evening Argus* optimistically reported that "champagne would be flowing at thirty thousand feet above America tomorrow as the Seagulls celebrate being Second Division champions".

TUESDAY 10TH MAY 1994

Nigel Martyn and Chris Armstrong both appeared as substitutes for England 'B' as they beat their Northern Irish counterparts 4-2 at Hillsborough in front of 8,258.

SATURDAY 10TH MAY 1997

Two late goals from Dougie Freedman helped Crystal Palace to a commanding 3-1 lead in the first leg of the play-off semi-final against Wolverhampton Wanderers.

SUNDAY 10TH MAY 1998

Crystal Palace signed off from a disastrous Premiership season that saw them relegated in April, by winning the last game of the campaign 1-0 against Sheffield Wednesday thanks to an injury-time strike from youngster Clinton Morrison after Lombardo provided the through-ball.

FRIDAY 11TH MAY 1979

Due to a postponed game, Crystal Palace played their last match of the 1978/79 season after the final fixtures. A balmy spring night saw a record attendance of 51,482 pack Selhurst Park hoping to see Terry Venables' men grab the single point needed for promotion to the First Division, or the win that would seal the title. Strikes from Ian Walsh and Dave Swindlehurst saw Burnley beaten 2-0 which ensured the Eagles finished top, displacing Brighton & Hove Albion in the process. Brighton were on their way to an end-of-season tour Stateside, and found out they had been pipped to the title courtesy of the pilot who revealed the result over the intercom.

WEDNESDAY 11TH MAY 1977

Crystal Palace travelled to fellow promotion candidates Wrexham knowing they must win to stand any chance of going up. The 20 year-old goalkeeper Peter Caswell was given his debut in place of the injured Tony Burns and George Graham was suspended. The Eagles took a two-goal lead, but were pegged back by Wrexham to 2-2. Incredibly, Rachid Harkouk scored with ninety seconds remaining before Jeff Bourne made it 4-2 moments later. Palace moved third and into the last promotion berth, with their fixtures finished, knowing that if Wrexham failed to beat champions-elect Mansfield Town in their last game they were up instead of the Welshmen.

SATURDAY 11TH MAY 1991

A brace from John Salako and the match opener from Ian Wright sealed a 3-0 win over Manchester United at Selhurst Park in the last game of the season. It was enough to hand Crystal Palace their best-ever finish of third in the top flight, a position Steve Coppell's men had held since December. But, would the Eagles be in the Uefa Cup next season or would Liverpool, who finished in second spot, be reinstated back into European competition at the expense of Palace?

TUESDAY 11TH MAY 2004

A plethora of legends gathered at Selhurst Park for Steve Kember's testimonial, which actually consisted of two matches; Crystal Palace Veterans versus Chelsea Veterans followed by the main event, the current Crystal Palace side taking on Crystal Palace All Stars, which featured the likes of Nigel Martyn, Ian Wright, Mark Bright and Clinton Morrison. The All Stars won 3-1, thanks to goals from Bruce Dyer, Phil Barber and Dean Gordon. Tyrone Berry netted for the current XI.

SATURDAY 12TH MAY 1990

Crystal Palace faced Manchester United in the 109th FA Cup Final, and the match was an absolute classic between two teams who both finished on 48 points in the First Division. Wembley was all-seated for the first time, and Palace fans had only been allocated 14,000 tickets out of the 80,000 available. But, they made their presence felt. The Eagles were welcomed onto the pitch with thousands of red and blue balloons. Gary O'Reilly put Palace in the lead after just 19 minutes, when his header looped over Jim Leighton in the United goal. Bryan Robson brought Alex Ferguson's men level before the break, thanks in part to John Pemberton's shin. Mark Hughes had the Reds ahead just after the hour, before the fairytale introduction of Ian Wright – who was touch and go for the bench due to recovering from a broken leg – on for Phil Barber after 69 minutes. With virtually his first touch of the ball, Wright had skipped clear of Mike Phelan, turned inside Gary Pallister and fired the ball hard and fast past the advancing Leighton to score one of the best goals Wembley had seen, whilst putting Palace level in the process. With the game into extra time, Wright grabbed his brace early on with another stunning effort. But Palace couldn't hold onto their lead, and just seven minutes from glory Mark Hughes made it 3-3 to force the replay.

SUNDAY 12TH MAY 1996

Crystal Palace won a first leg of the play-off semi-final 2-1 at Charlton Athletic thanks to strikes from Kenny Brown and Carl Veart.

SATURDAY 13TH MAY 1967

Crystal Palace beat Wolves 4-1 on the final day of the season, which secured a credible seventh place finish in the Second Division. The result, in front of 26,930 at Selhurst Park, also meant the Midlands side missed out on the title and had to settle for second spot.

SUNDAY 13TH MAY 1956

Palace legend Johnny Byrne signed professional forms for the Glaziers on his 17th birthday. Born in West Horsley in Surrey, Byrne played for Howard of Effingham School, Epsom Town and Guildford City before being recommended to Palace by former keeper Vic Blore.

SATURDAY 13TH MAY 1989

Yet again Crystal Palace entered the final day of the season with something resting on the outcome, this time outright promotion. A convincing win over relegated Birmingham City at Selhurst Park, coupled with rivals Manchester City losing to Bradford City would see Coppell's men back in the big time. Palace made an excellent start, Ian Wright scoring in the 13th minute but the game was then held up for 27 minutes as Birmingham fans started fighting and spilling onto the pitch. Blues boss Dave Mackay had to make a touchline appeal for calm as the mounted police herded the fans back into the away end. On resumption of the contest, Wright bagged two more to get a first half hat-trick and an Ian Clarkson own goal meant Palace went in 4-0 at the break. But as news came through during the second half that Manchester City had gained the point that they needed for second spot and automatic promotion, Palace tailed off and allowed Birmingham a consolation.

TUESDAY 13TH MAY 2008

Neil Warnock just missed out on taking the Eagles to the play-off final after just seven months in charge, when Bristol City broke Palace hearts with a win after extra time in the second leg of the semi-final at Ashton Gate. Ben Watson had levelled the tie when he put Palace ahead in the 24th minute, only for Lee Trundle and Michael McIndoe to score in the 104th and 110th minutes respectively.

WEDNESDAY 14TH MAY 1969

Crystal Palace headed off to Spain on tour as a reward for promotion to the top flight. Benidorm were first, and were beaten 4-2.

SATURDAY 14TH MAY 1977

With Crystal Palace having completed their league fixtures and sat in the last remaining promotion spot, Eagles fans kept an eye on results elsewhere to see if they would be watching Division Two football the following season. Mansfield scored a late winner to beat Wrexham 1-0 at the Racecourse Ground which sealed the Third Division title for the Stags and kept the Robins in fourth, one point behind Palace. Rotherham United beat Port Vale 4-1 away, ending on the same points as Palace, but superior goal difference meant Terry Venables' men went up instead. Brighton & Hove Albion finished second and were also promoted!

MONDAY 14TH MAY 1984

Alan Mullery was sacked for the first time in his managerial career after Ron Noades wielded the axe following two seasons of decline under the former England international.

SUNDAY 14TH MAY 1995

Crystal Palace went up to St James' Park for the last game of the season against Newcastle United knowing they needed a win and results elsewhere to go their way if they were to stay in the top flight. But when Newcastle banged in the earliest goal of the Premiership that afternoon, the 1,000 or so Palace fans who made the trip knew the game was up. The Eagles lost 3-2 and ended the season three points from Aston Villa and safety. Any other season Palace would have been safe finishing fourth from bottom, but with the Premiership being reduced from 22 to 20 clubs the following campaign, the bottom four spots were all relegation berths.

WEDNESDAY 14TH MAY 1997

Crystal Palace lost 2-1 to Wolverhampton Wanderers at a hostile Molineux in the second leg of the play-off semi-final, but the hard work had already been done at Selhurst and the Eagles went through to Wembley thanks to a 4-3 aggregate win. David Hopkin scored the decisive goal in the Black Country, beating two defenders before smashing the ball into the net from the edge of the area.

FRIDAY 14TH MAY 2004

Goals from Neil Shipperley, Danny Butterfield and Andy Johnson gave Crystal Palace a slender 3-2 victory over Sunderland in the first leg of the play-off semi-final at Selhurst Park.

SATURDAY 15TH MAY 1982

Palace finished their Second Division campaign with a defeat to Newcastle United in front of 8,453 at Selhurst Park. The Eagles ended up 15th overall, which was precisely the position they were in when Steve Kember took over from Dario Gradi in November 1981.

MONDAY 15TH MAY 1995

Alan Smith left Crystal Palace by mutual consent after the Eagles dropped out of the Premiership after just one season.

WEDNESDAY 15TH MAY 1996

Crystal Palace skipper Ray Houghton scored after just four minutes at Selhurst Park in the second leg of the play-off semi-final against Charlton Athletic to take the score to 3-1 on aggregate. The Addicks huffed and puffed for the rest of the game but they couldn't stop the Eagles going to Wembley for the play-off final.

SUNDAY 15TH MAY 2005

Crystal Palace fell at the very last hurdle in their quest to stay in the Premiership, when just eight minutes from time, Jon Fortune's header gave Charlton a 2-2 draw and condemned Palace to their fourth relegation in 14 years from the top flight. Andy Johnson had given Palace the lead with his 21st goal of the season in the 71st minute following Dougie Freedman's leveller, but it was to no avail. However, with that goal "AJ" was the Premiership's second highest scorer, second only to Thierry Henry, and was widely lauded for being the top scoring Englishman in one of the world's toughest leagues.

SATURDAY 16TH MAY 1908

Crystal Palace embarked on their first overseas tour venturing to Prague, then part of the Austro-Hungarian Empire. Slavia were beaten three times, whilst victories over Snnichow, Koniggratz and Kladno ensured Edmund Goodman's men returned home with a 100% record.

SATURDAY 17TH MAY 1947

New Crystal Palace manager Jack Butler, who joined from Torquay United, started off on a losing note in his first game in charge as his men lost 1-0 away at Northampton in the league. The former Arsenal centre-half and England international replaced George Irwin who had steered The Glaziers to three wartime league championships.

SATURDAY 17TH MAY 1941

Crystal Palace recorded their biggest victory of the season when they beat Southend United 7-0 at Selhurst Park. The opposition goalkeeper had such a bad time, he stormed off the pitch after letting in a goal forcing the Southend centre-forward to don the green jersey and get between the sticks. The result ultimately helped Palace win the wartime championship ahead of West Ham in second spot and Arsenal in third, as the league positions were decided purely on goal average. Due to difficulties of travel at the time, clubs were free to play as many or as few games as they chose. Palace met Arsenal both home and away, drawing both games, but never faced West Ham.

TUESDAY 17TH MAY 1983

Four years after facing Burnley at home on the last day of the season to get promoted out of the Second Division, Palace faced the Clarets knowing they could be relegated to the Third Division. A crowd of 22,714 – almost three times the average gate – witnessed Ian Edwards guide the ball home just after the hour to give the Eagles a 1-0 win and guarantee safety. Mullery's men finished one point above Chelsea, who themselves escaped the drop.

THURSDAY 17TH MAY 1984

Dave "Harry" Bassett was appointed Crystal Palace manager following the sacking of Alan Mullery three days earlier.

MONDAY 17TH MAY 1993

After seeing Crystal Palace get relegated from the Premier League, Steve Coppell went on a brief holiday before handing in his resignation for the first time as Palace manager, despite having another year left on his contract.

MONDAY 17TH MAY 2004

A night of pure drama up at the Stadium of Light in the second leg of the play-off semi-final against Sunderland, as Crystal Palace squeezed through on penalties to the showpiece at the Millennium Stadium, Cardiff. Iain Dowie's men had looked dead and buried when the Black Cats were 2-0 up on the night and 4-3 on aggregate but they hadn't reckoned on Darren Powell bundling home in the dying seconds to level the scores overall, and ultimately take the game to the shoot-out. Michael Hughes was the man who slotted home the pressure kick, after an agonising 13 penalties had already been taken.

FRIDAY 18TH MAY 1979

The *Croydon Advertiser* reported that chairman Ray Bloye had done a deal to lease the land behind the Whitehorse Lane end to supermarket chain Sainsbury's in order to secure the club's future. It later emerged a 99-year lease had changed hands for £2m.

WEDNESDAY 19TH MAY 1976

Malcolm Allison resigned after failing to get promotion from the Third Division, and failing to reach the FA Cup Final, having gone so close.

SATURDAY 19TH MAY 2007

Crystal Palace USA recorded their first-ever competitive win, beating Wilmington Hammerheads 3-0 in front of 3,417 at the Legion Sports Complex thanks to strikes from Sergio Flores, Andrew Marshall and Josh Alcala.

MONDAY 21ST MAY 1984

After just four days at the helm, Dave Bassett quit Crystal Palace as manager and returned to Wimbledon. The fans were inevitably concerned with what was going on behind the scenes at the club for someone to turn on their heels so quickly.

SUNDAY 21ST MAY 1989

Having finished third in the Second Division, Crystal Palace were involved in the play-offs for the very first time in their history. In the heat of the County Ground, Palace lost 1-0 to Swindon Town in the first leg after an unfortunate own goal from Jeff Hopkins.

WEDNESDAY 22ND MAY 1963

Crystal Palace beat Barnsley 4-0 to finish 11th in the Third Division, having been second to bottom at Christmas. Teams had to play three games in four days just to get the league completed by the end of May, thanks to a harsh winter that saw scores of postponed fixtures.

TUESDAY 23RD MAY 2006

Iain Dowie left Crystal Palace by mutual consent in order to spend more time with his wife and two sons, who lived near Bolton. The morning papers revealed that Dowie had also pointedly refused to rule out working in the south-east of England again in the near future. This prompted Simon Jordan to joke that he would "not be very happy" if the former Palace striker was to do such a thing and join one of their rivals.

WEDNESDAY 24TH MAY 1989

The Wright and Bright show continued as both strikers grabbed a goal at Selhurst Park in the second leg of the play-off semi-final to help Crystal Palace ease past Swindon Town 2-1 on aggregate, overturning a one goal deficit from the first leg.

WEDNESDAY 24TH MAY 2006

Crystal Palace confirmed that a bid of £8.5 million had been accepted from Wigan Athletic for striker Andrew Johnson.

SATURDAY 24TH MAY 2003

Steve Kember was officially made Crystal Palace manager having been put in caretaker charge after Trevor Francis had left.

WEDNESDAY 25TH MAY 2005

Pictures came through from America of Andrew Johnson training with the England squad at the Illinois Institute of Technology ahead of their friendly against the USA three days later in Chicago.

THURSDAY 25TH MAY 2006

Crystal Palace accepted a bid of £8.5 million from Bolton Wanderers for Andrew Johnson, as the striker was named as a substitute for the England 'B' game against Belarus at the Madejski stadium in Reading the same night.

IAN WRIGHT

MONDAY 26TH MAY 1997

Crystal Palace faced Sheffield United in the Division One play-off final at Wembley with the winner taking their place in the top flight the next season. Howard Kendall's United had beaten Palace in both league encounters earlier on in the campaign but they weren't about to make it third time lucky. Chances were few and far between in a match played out in the blistering heat in front of 64,383, but with the last quarter of an hour to go Palace fans made a concerted effort to raise their players on the pitch with a thunderous cacophony of constant chanting, cheering and clapping. It worked, for in the 89th minute recently voted for Player Of The Year David Hopkin found the ball dropping to him 22 yards out from United's goal following Carl Tiler's clearing header for the Blades. Unmarked, the Scottish midfielder was able to return the ball with interest, lashing home an unstoppable shot that flew into the top right-hand corner. Palace won 1-0 and Steve Coppell had successfully returned to take the Eagles back to the promised land of the Premiership.

MONDAY 27TH MAY 1996

A day Crystal Palace fans will want to forget as Steve Claridge's shin looped the ball over Nigel Martyn and into the back of the net in the dying seconds of extra time to give Leicester City a 2-1 win in the play-off final and promotion to the Premiership. The match had started so well for Palace, as Andy Roberts had given the Eagles a 14th minute lead, only for Garry Parker to tuck home a 76th minute penalty to level matters after a foul on Muzzy Izzet. With the game fizzling out to a 1-1 draw, Foxes manager Martin O'Neill bought on 6ft 7in keeper Zeljko Kalac to try and seek an advantage in the inevitable penalty shoot-out. But it never came, as former Palace reserve striker Claridge stuck out his leg and got lucky, to the delight of the East Midlanders in the 73,573 crowd at Wembley.

SATURDAY 28TH MAY 2006

Tony Popovic was named in the Australian squad for their friendly against New Zealand at Craven Cottage on Thursday 9th June as a warm-up for the FIFA Confederations Cup in Germany – he later played in the game to reach 50 caps for his country.

SATURDAY 28TH MAY 2005

Andrew Johnson made his full debut for England, starting in the 2-1 win over the USA in Chicago.

SATURDAY 29TH MAY 2004

The 2003/04 season came down to one game at Cardiff's Millennium Stadium, with just Alan Pardew's West Ham standing in the way of Crystal Palace's return to the Premiership. The Hammers went into the game the favourites, but it would be Palace who walked away with the supposed £30m windfall that came with membership of the top flight of English football, thanks to a simple tap-in from skipper Neil Shipperley after a searching run and shot from Andy Johnson had stung West Ham keeper Stephen Bywater into parrying the ball to his feet – 1-0 to Palace, and the Eagles went back to where they belonged. The John Harbin ethos of treating the match as simply "one more round" had paid off magnificently against an opposition who on the day pompously wore T-shirts bearing the slogan "The Original Academy".

TUESDAY 30TH MAY 2006

Iain Dowie was unveiled as the new head coach of Charlton Athletic but the press conference descended into farce when a bailiff acting on behalf of Simon Jordan issued the former Crystal Palace manager with a high court writ for misrepresenting his reasons for leaving Selhurst Park. Palace's claim for damages centred on a series of private conversations between Jordan and Dowie just prior to his departure on May 22. Jordan alleged that Dowie lied about his reasons for wanting to end his contract and that Palace consequently waived a £1m compensation settlement which would have applied had he resigned to take over at another club.

TUESDAY 31ST MAY 1977

Crystal Palace centre-back Ian Evans enjoyed his finest moment as an international when he helped Wales to a 1-0 win over England at Wembley in front of 48,000 in the Home Championship. It was the Principality's first victory over England since 1955 and their first on English soil for over forty years.

WEDNESDAY 31st MAY 1989

Crystal Palace faced Blackburn over two legs in the play-off final after Rovers sneaked through on away goals against Watford. But the first leg did not go too well up at Ewood Park, Howard Gayle putting Don Mackay's team 2-0 up midway through the second half. Gayle then missed out on a hat-trick when he fired a penalty wide, and when Eddie McGoldrick halved the deficit four minutes from time Steve Coppell thought he had got away with an "alright result", only for Simon Garner to nick one at the death, which restored Rovers' two goal advantage ahead of the Selhurst Park game.

THURSDAY 31st MAY 2001

Steve Kember may have been a popular choice to take on the role of manager full-time after securing Crystal Palace's Division One status, but Simon Jordan opted to employ former Norwich City and Manchester United captain Steve Bruce, who had previously managed Sheffield United, Huddersfield Town and Wigan Athletic.

CRYSTAL PALACE
On This Day

JUNE

SATURDAY 1st JUNE 1991

John Salako made his debut for England, coming on as a half-time replacement for Sheffield Wednesday striker David Hirst in a friendly against Australia in the Sydney football stadium watched by 35,472 fans. Geoff Thomas collected his fourth cap when he started in midfield as Graham Taylor's men won 1-0 thanks to a 41st minute own goal from Ian Gray. The England starting line-up was: Chris Woods, Paul Parker, Stuart Pearce, David Batty, Des Walker, Mark Wright, David Platt, Geoff Thomas, Nigel Clough, Gary Lineker and David Hirst with Dennis Wise coming on for Lineker in the 81st minute.

TUESDAY 1st JUNE 1976

Terry Venables was promoted from coach to manager of Crystal Palace in the wake of Malcolm Allison's departure.

TUESDAY 1st JUNE 1982

Alan Mullery resigned from Charlton Athletic after less than a year in the job when Addicks chairman Michael Gliksten told him the club didn't want First Division football as it would create more financial problems. The very same day Ron Noades dismissed Steve Kember as manager of Crystal Palace. Kember learnt of his fate whilst on holiday.

MONDAY 2nd JUNE 1958

Brighton & Hove Albion attempted a close season raid on Crystal Palace for their promising youngster Johnny Byrne by offering £10,000, along with journeymen inside-forwards Johnny Shepherd and Denis Foreman. The Selhurst Park board weren't unwilling to do business, but they asked the south coast outfit to increase their offer. Brighton baulked, and in the process missed the chance to rob their rivals of their best player for generations.

FRIDAY 2nd JUNE 2006

England international Andrew Johnson completed his £8.6m move from Crystal Palace to Everton, having served up 84 goals for the Palace faithful during his time at Selhurst Park. At Goodison, AJ started brightly but starts became limited with the arrival of Yakubu, and Johnson was transferred to Fulham in August 2008 for £10.5m, having scored 17 goals in 52 league starts for the Toffees.

SATURDAY 3RD JUNE 1989

"Play-offs are cruel but our performance here was nothing short of magnificent," was Steve Coppell's summing up as Crystal Palace beat Blackburn Rovers 4-3 on aggregate to return to the top flight. But the Eagles had to do it the hard way, going into the match 3-1 down after the first leg. An expectant Selhurst Park capacity crowd of 30,000, nearly double the attendance at Ewood Park, got the early goal they wished for when Ian Wright bundled home at the second attempt for his 32nd strike of the season. Just after the break Eddie McGoldrick went down under Mark Atkins' clumsy challenge and referee George Courtney pointed to the spot. Dave Madden stepped up to fire the 47th minute penalty home in front of the Whitehorse Lane End and take the score to 3-3 overall in the tie. The tie went to extra time, and if Coppell's men could hold on they would be promoted having scored the solitary away goal. But it never needed to come into play, as two minutes from time Wright rose unchallenged to head home McGoldrick's cross to spark an ecstatic pitch invasion. Palace were back in the big time, and in some style.

MONDAY 3RD JUNE 1991

Two days after his first international cap, John Salako won his second when England played their first ever game against New Zealand, a friendly at Mount Smart in Auckland, in front of a crowd of 17,520. On as a 70th minute substitute for Rangers' Mark Walters, Salako tasted victory – alongside club team-mate Geoff Thomas who started the match to add cap number five in the process – when Gary Lineker grabbed the only goal of the game in the 90th minute.

THURSDAY 3RD JUNE 1993

Alan Smith was installed as the new Crystal Palace manager, stepping up from assistant manager, in the wake of Steve Coppell's resignation following relegation. Smith immediately made it clear that he would adopt a different style of football as he attempted to get Palace back into the Premier League: "I've decided to use a pass-and-move style this season. People don't want to see the ball being constantly pumped through the middle."

MONDAY 4TH JUNE 1984

One of the greatest days in the history of Crystal Palace as Steve Coppell was appointed manager. Coppell had no idea who he wanted as his assistant, so agreed to go with Ron Noades' suggestion of Ian Evans.

FRIDAY 4TH JUNE 1971

Crystal Palace turned up at the San Siro to take on Inter Milan in the Anglo-Italian Inter-League Clubs' Competition. Inter, who were the Italian champions and had not lost since the previous November, were beaten 2-1 by the South Londoners thanks to a stunning Bobby Tambling brace.

SUNDAY 5TH JUNE 1938

Future Crystal Palace manager Jack Butler saw his Belgium side crash out of the 1938 World Cup in the first round at the hands of the hosts, France. Alfred Aston, the French right-winger with an English father, inspired his team to a 3-1 victory in front of 30,000 at the Stade Olympique in Colombes, Paris.

MONDAY 6TH JUNE 2005

Tom Soares featured for England under-20s in their 3-0 win over South Korea at the Stade Scaglia in La Seyne to send them into the semi-final of the Toulon Tournament. Soares was eventually replaced by David Nugent of Preston North End in the 59th minute. Peter Taylor was the manager, and Scott Flinders, then of Barnsley, featured in goal.

SUNDAY 7TH JUNE 1992

Eddie McGoldrick came on for Terry Phelan in the 89th minute as the Republic of Ireland beat Portugal 2-0 in the Foxboro Stadium, Boston, USA in front of 41,227 in the inaugural US Cup tournament that also featured the USA and Italy.

SATURDAY 8TH JUNE 1991

Palace had three players in the England starting line-up for the friendly against New Zealand at Athletic Park in Wellington, more than any other club. John Salako made his full debut alongside Ian Wright and Geoff Thomas as the Eagles trio played the full 90 minutes. Goals from Stuart Pearce and David Hirst ensured a 2-0 win for Graham Taylor's team.

MONDAY 8TH JUNE 1981

Somewhat inevitably, Clive Allen continued the exodus of players moving from Crystal Palace to QPR in an exchange deal that saw 6ft 3ins centre-half Steve Wicks moving the other way. The deal was valued at £675,000.

MONDAY 8TH JUNE 1987

Future England midfielder Geoff Thomas signed for Palace from Crewe Alexandra for £50,000. It turned out to be a real bargain.

THURSDAY 8TH JUNE 1995

Steve Coppell came back to Crystal Palace in the strategic post of Technical Director, overseeing Ray Lewington and Peter Nicholas who looked after the playing side of the first team.

SATURDAY 9TH JUNE 2007

Crystal Palace USA beat the Charlotte Eagles 1-0 thanks to Charlie Sheringham's 9th minute strike. Sheringham, son of striker Teddy Sheringham, was on loan from Crystal Palace USA's parent club.

WEDNESDAY 10TH JUNE 1998

Mark Goldberg completed his takeover of Crystal Palace earlier than the October hand-over due to Ron Noades being linked with a move to Brentford. Goldberg soon announced that Terry Venables was to be the Eagles' new head coach in a widely anticipated move.

MONDAY 11TH JUNE 2006

Crystal Palace announced a press conference would be taking place at 4pm – speculation suggested it would be former player Peter Taylor who would be announced as the new manager of the Eagles. Palace later unveiled Taylor as the new manager, who joined from Hull City having previously managed Brighton & Hove Albion.

TUESDAY 12TH JUNE 2007

Crystal Palace USA suffered a shock 1-0 defeat at the hands of the Ocean City Barons in the US Open Cup in a bad-tempered game.

FRIDAY 13TH JUNE 1980

Arsenal paid QPR £1.25m for young striker Clive Allen, after he scored 32 goals in 49 games for the West London outfit. Allen moved to Crystal Palace just two months later.

THURSDAY 14TH JUNE 2007

Crystal Palace chairman Simon Jordan scored a legal victory after a high court judge upheld his claim that he was "deceived" by manager Iain Dowie over his reasons for walking away from the club. Jordan had previously accused Dowie of telling lies when he negotiated his way out of his contract with Palace, as he went on to join arch-rivals Charlton Athletic rather than move back to his family in the north-west of England. Mr Justice Tugendhat ruled that Palace had entered into a compromise agreement with Dowie on the basis of his "fraudulent representations". Dowie had a clause in his contract to the effect that, if he left to directly join another club, Palace would receive £1m compensation. "I took a man to the high court for fraudulent misrepresentation, and he's been found guilty," stated Jordan. "I think it's a good day for football because managers' contracts and what people do and say in football are very important. And I think that having the courage of your convictions to take it to the high court and bring an action – a very difficult action to prove, fraudulent misrepresentation – and be successful, is a good thing. So I am pleased from that perspective." Dowie, who spoke through a statement released through his new club Coventry City, admitted the outcome was not the one he had wanted but vowed to put the case behind him. "Obviously this is a hugely disappointing result for myself and my family," he stated. "The whole experience has been a very testing time but it is not something I will allow to destroy my determination to succeed at Coventry City, who I am fully committed to."

THURSDAY 15TH JUNE 1995

Marc Edworthy signed for Crystal Palace in a £350,000 transfer from Plymouth Argyle. The defender made 151 appearances scoring just once.

MONDAY 15TH JUNE 1998

Ron Noades left Crystal Palace ahead of his October hand-over to Mark Goldberg in order to purchase Brentford from former owner Dave Webb. Noades immediately appointed Palace coach Ray Lewington in a similar role at Griffin Park.

MONDAY 16TH JUNE 2008

Carlos Morales became the first Crystal Palace USA player to receive an international call-up when Puerto Rico selected him in their squad for their World Cup qualifier against Honduras.

SATURDAY 16TH JUNE 2007

Crystal Palace USA beat Bermuda Hogges 2-1 at the Navy-Marine Corps Stadium thanks to strikes from Matthew Mbuta and Josh Alcala.

FRIDAY 17TH JUNE 2005

Crystal Palace announced that they had agreed an undisclosed compensation fee with Tottenham Hotspur for 20-year-old Wayne Routledge, who would join Spurs on July 1st 2005. Routledge made 123 appearances for the Eagles.

MONDAY 17TH JUNE 2002

Crystal Palace defender Greg Berhalter became the first Palace player to appear in a World Cup when he started for the USA in their last 16 game against Mexico in front of 36,380 at the Jeonju Stadium in South Korea. Goals from Brian McBride and Landon Donovan eased the States through to the quarter-finals at the expense of their neighbours.

SUNDAY 18TH JUNE 2006

Australian defender Tony Popovic became the second-ever current Crystal Palace player to appear in a World Cup when he started the late afternoon Group F match against eventual quarter-finalists Brazil at the Allianz Arena in Munich, Germany. Unfortunately, 'Poppa' was forced to leave the field with a calf injury after 40 minutes, with the scores level at 0-0. The game finished 2-0 to the South Americans whose starting line-up was Dida, Cafu, Lucio, Juan, Roberto Carlos, Kaka, Emerson, Ze Roberto, Ronaldinho, Ronaldo and Adriano.

SUNDAY 19TH JUNE 2005

Crystal Palace midfielder Vassilis Lakis played in Greece's 1-0 defeat to Japan in a group B match in the Confederations Cup at Frankfurt's Waldstadion.

TUESDAY 20TH JUNE 2006

The club asked fans if they would be interested in an organised club tour to the USA to see the first-ever game between Crystal Palace and their American team in a pre-season friendly.

TUESDAY 20TH JUNE 2006

News came through that Tony Popovic had been ruled out of Australia's final World Cup Group F match against Croatia on Thursday 23rd June. Born in Australia, Popovic was nonetheless desperate to face his country of descent but his calf injury, picked up against Brazil, proved too much. Australian assistant coach Graham Arnold said missing the game was "hurting him very badly".

THURSDAY 21ST JUNE 2001

Following a month of speculation Crystal Palace named Steve Bruce as their new manager, despite George Graham, Alan Pardew and Joe Royle all being linked with the job. Chairman Simon Jordan proclaimed: "This is a new era for us and not an FAlse dawn – I believe Steve Bruce has the focus, commitment and leadership to make us successful."

FRIDAY 21ST JUNE 2002

It was the end of Crystal Palace's interest in the World Cup as Germany knocked out the USA at the quarter-final stage, the Americans having fielded Selhurst Park defender Greg Berhalter.

THURSDAY 22ND JUNE 2006

Crystal Palace cancelled their American friendly game against Virginia Beach Mariners, scheduled to take place a month later, when the opposition club went out of business.

THURSDAY 22ND JUNE 2006

Australia drew 2-2 with Croatia in their Group F World Cup game in Stuttgart, which confirmed their qualification for the next round. Infamously, it was the game where referee Graham Poll showed Josip Simunic *three* yellow cards. Crystal Palace and Socceroos defender Tony Popovic had to watch from the stands as he was injured, but insisted he would be back: "I should be OK for the second round – I'm not ready to come home yet and the game against Brazil gave me a taste for more."

FRIDAY 23RD JUNE 2006

New boss Peter Taylor stated that the forthcoming season would see "46 hard games," but that he was "looking forward to my first home game in charge of Palace as it's against my old team, Southend United".

THURSDAY 24TH JUNE 1982

In his wisdom, Ron Noades decided to appoint Alan Mullery as the new manager of Crystal Palace. The former Brighton & Hove Albion gaffer looked for a quick return to work after resigning from Charlton Athletic. Whilst Noades believed Mullery could operate successfully on a shoestring budget as he had done at his previous clubs, the fans weren't happy. Many vowed never to set foot inside Selhurst Park whilst he was there, citing Mullery's antics during the infamous FA Cup replay at Stamford Bridge in 1976.

MONDAY 25TH JUNE 1946

Future Brighton & Hove Albion manager Chris Cattlin was born in Lancashire, and thankfully for Crystal Palace fans, he later went on to reject a trialist by the name of Ian Wright from Penge Sunday League outfit Ten Em Bee, in favour of Steve Penney.

SUNDAY 26TH JUNE 1994

Midfielder Andy Preece signed for Crystal Palace from Stockport County for £350,000. In 20 league games Preece scored four times before moving to Blackpool.

WEDNESDAY 27TH JUNE 2007

Crystal Palace raided near neighbours Millwall for defender Tony Craig, who made 13 league starts before he moved back to The New Den.

WEDNESDAY 28TH JUNE 2000

Craig Foster turned out for Australia as they took on neighbours New Zealand in an Oceania Nations Cup fixture in front of 2,000 fans in Papeete, Tahiti. The Socceroos won 2-0 with Foster bagging the second.

FRIDAY 29TH JUNE 2007

Crystal Palace USA drew away against Cleveland City Stars. Larry Mark scored an 86th minute equaliser at the Krenzler Stadium.

FRIDAY 30TH JUNE 1978

QPR finally got their man when they tempted Rachid Harkouk to Loftus Road. Crystal Palace were handed £90,000 in the process. Born in Chelsea of an Algerian father and a Yorkshire mother, "Spider" made 63 appearances for Palace scoring 25 times.

MONDAY 30TH JUNE 1958

Manager Cyril Spiers left Crystal Palace after he failed to avoid the drop into the newly-formed Fourth Division. George Smith, previously in charge of Eastbourne and Sutton United was appointed the new manager soon after with Arthur Rowe as his assistant. Rowe had managed Spurs to their first ever First Division title in 1950/51 with his widely acclaimed "push and run" football and had recently returned to the game after a spell away due to ill health.

TUESDAY 30TH JUNE 1936

After less than a year in the job, Crystal Palace manager Tom Bromilow tendered his resignation after a boardroom re-shuffle at Selhurst Park left him exasperated. Bizarrely, Bromilow was succeeded by one of the directors, Mr R S Moyes, whose stay was to prove both short and turbulent.

FRIDAY 30TH JUNE 1995

Tottenham Hotspur paid Crystal Palace a then club record fee of £4.5m for striker Chris Armstrong. He became the first player to leave the relegated Eagles.

CRYSTAL PALACE
On This Day

JULY

SUNDAY 1st JULY 1979

Crystal Palace paid a club record fee of £465,000 to QPR for England star Gerry Francis. Unfortunately, the Chiswick-born midfielder had already played his last game for his country, having captained England to a 4-1 win away to Finland in a World Cup qualifier in June 1976. A niggling back injury kept Francis out after that and he never regained his place.

SATURDAY 1st JULY 1995

Aston Villa stepped in to take Gareth Southgate back to the Premiership when they paid £2.5m for his services.

TUESDAY 2nd JULY 1996

Palace missed out on the transfer targets of Bristol Rovers striker Marcus Stewart and Huddersfield Town's Andy Booth, who moved to Huddersfield Town and Sheffield Wednesday respectively.

WEDNESDAY 3rd JULY 1996

Millwall's highly-rated defender Ben Thatcher moved to Wimbledon, over Crystal Palace, in a £2m transfer.

FRIDAY 4th JULY 2008

Neil Warnock began rebuilding for the 2008/09 season when he made the double capture of Darryl Flahavan from Southend United and Johannes Ertl from Austria Wien.

WEDNESDAY 5th JULY 2000

Whitehorse Lane born-and-bred super fan Simon Jordan saved Crystal Palace when he bought the club for £10.5m. The deal wasn't entirely simple though, as Jordan had to purchase the club off Gerry Lim immediately after the Singaporean financier had acquired it. Lim himself had earlier struck a deal with the administrators to buy the club, but had grown frustrated at how long it was taking to complete. It was at this point that the Crystal Palace Supporters' Trust stepped in to introduce Lim to Jordan, who wasn't getting anywhere with his own direct dealings with the administrators. The two men spoke, and as a result of those talks Crystal Palace Football Club lived on with Jordan as the new owner.

MONDAY 6TH JULY 1998

Terry Fenwick returned to Palace as Terry Venables' coach. Venables was absent from most of pre-season training due to TV commitments so Fenwick took most of the sessions at the new facilities at Streete Court.

SATURDAY 7TH JULY 2007

Crystal Palace USA lost 1-0 at home to the Western Mass Pioneers in the league.

SUNDAY 8TH JULY 2001

The Crystal Palace first-team squad left Beckenham for their Spanish pre-season tour.

SATURDAY 8TH JULY 2006

Palace launched their new kits for the forthcoming season, with the traditional red and blue stripes featuring for the home kit and an unusual grey and white swirl for the away kit. Made by Diadora, the shirts featured a new logo from club sponsors GAC Logistics.

WEDNESDAY 9TH JULY 1997

Crystal Palace started their pre-season tour of Finland with a convincing 4-0 win over JJK thanks to a hat-trick from Gareth Davies and a strike from Scottish hitman Dougie Freedman.

WEDNESDAY 10TH JULY 1996

Ray Lewington took Palace's first-year professionals on a lung-bursting run through Richmond Park.

TUESDAY 11TH JULY 2006

Crystal Palace announced the signing, on a two-year contract, of 30-year-old midfielder Mark Kennedy from Wolves. The out-of-contract former Millwall and Liverpool player stated: "Once I knew Crystal Palace were interested and had heard what they were offering I had no hesitations whatsoever in coming back down to London."

FRIDAY 12TH JULY 1996

Manager Dave Bassett was on holiday, but the press still linked Niall Quinn, Brian Deane and Paul Rideout with moves to Selhurst Park.

THURSDAY 13TH JULY 2000

Crystal Palace made their first permanent signings since November 1998, when Arsenal's highly-rated youngsters Tommy Black and Julian Gray were snapped up.

FRIDAY 13TH JULY 2007

Crystal Palace USA drew 0-0 at the Skyline Sports Complex against the Harrisburg City Islanders.

FRIDAY 13TH JULY 2007

Manager Peter Taylor returned to Essex as his Crystal Palace first team faced Chelmsford City in their first pre-season friendly of the campaign. Dougie Freedman scored a brace as Palace won 2-0.

SATURDAY 14TH JULY 2007

Peter Taylor's Crystal Palace drew 2-2 with Bromley at Hayes Lane in front of 3,148. Paul Ifill, and an own goal, helped Palace to a draw.

SATURDAY 15TH JULY 2006

In his second game in charge of Crystal Palace, Peter Taylor faced the newly-formed Palace USA team co-managed by Jim Cherneski and Pete Medd at the US Naval Academy ground in Annapolis, Maryland. South London Palace cantered to a 3-1 win over their American counterparts, but Rade Kokovic went down in Palace USA history as the first-ever goalscorer in *any* game for the fledgling Stateside outfit.

TUESDAY 15TH JULY 1997

Ron Noades rubbished reports linking Roberto Baggio of AC Milan with Crystal Palace but revealed that the Lombardo deal was still possible. One player who did sign was goalkeeper Kevin Miller, who joined from Watford for £1.25m with Chris Day going to Vicarage Road. On the playing side, Palace beat Santa Claus of Finland 5-0.

MONDAY 16TH JULY 2007

Crystal Palace USA travelled to the island of Bermuda and beat former Manchester City player Shaun Goater's team, the Bermuda Hogges, 2-1 at the National Stadium.

PETER TAYLOR RETURNS TO PALACE AS BOSS

SATURDAY 17TH JULY 2004

Andy Johnson grabbed a hat-trick as Crystal Palace beat Glentoran 5-0 on the pre-season tour of Northern Ireland.

WEDNESDAY 16TH JULY 2008

Simon Jordan expressed his intention to sell Crystal Palace in the forthcoming year, having believed he had taken the club as far as he could. Disillusionment with the game of football following the John Bostock affair was also an FActor. Jordan stated: "It's my specific intention to find a buyer this season. I will do nothing to affect manager Neil Warnock and I will be absolutely committed to the club and I will find a responsible buyer. I am not de-motivated by the team, manager or fans. But I have been disillusioned with football for a long time. I kept my sanity by pumping millions of pounds into my academy, feeling the saving grace of my club was finding players who would be chomping at the bit and honoured to play in the first team. But that's been taken away from me as well. Bostock was one of the best players my academy has produced in the last 10 years – and he has been sold for a packet of crisps. Bostock was the gem of gems and had Manchester United and Barcelona courting him. I got £700,000 by the tribunal – the system that is meant to represent me."

SATURDAY 18TH JULY 1992

Crystal Palace became the first international football club to visit a post-apartheid South Africa when they embarked on a mini pre-season tour. First up on the fixture list were the Kaizer Chiefs who the Eagles beat 3-2 in Johannesburg. The next day, Palace faced Orlando Pirates in Durban and went down 2-1.

FRIDAY 18TH JULY 1997

It was announced that Mark Goldberg had joined the Crystal Palace board with the intention of helping develop Selhurst Park into a super stadium and leisure complex, as well as providing funds for new players.

FRIDAY 19TH JULY 1991

Steve Coppell signed Welsh under-21 defender Chris Coleman from Swansea for £275,000.

SUNDAY 19TH JULY 1998

Crystal Palace played their first-ever game in European competition, when they entertained Turkish side Samsunspor in the third round, first leg of the Uefa Intertoto Cup. Terry Fenwick took charge of the side as Terry Venables fancied a holiday after being away commentating on the World Cup. The game kicked-off fifteen minutes late as more fans than expected turn up. The Eagles missed a late penalty as the Turks took charge of the tie, winning 2-0 in front of 7,943 at Selhurst Park.

WEDNESDAY 19TH JULY 2006

In the second and final match of a brief tour of the USA, Peter Taylor's men faced MLS champions LA Galaxy at the University of Richmond, Virginia. Galaxy coach Frank Yallop, who played for Ipswich Town, was able to play USA internationals Chris Albright and Cobi Jones, once of Coventry City, and Jamaican international defender Tyrone Marshall against Crystal Palace. The game itself saw the Eagles go 1-0 up thanks to a Jon Macken strike after just five minutes. Former Arsenal trainee Paulo Nagamura then slipped the ball past Julian Speroni to equalise for the Californians, but the worsening storm conditions forced the referee to abandon the game at half-time, the score standing at 1-1.

FRIDAY 20TH JULY 2007

Crystal Palace USA beat the Western Mass Pioneers 1-0 at the Lusitano Stadium.

WEDNESDAY 20TH JULY 2005

Palace lost their first pre-season match in Germany, going down 2-1 against FK Teplice, despite an Andrew Johnson penalty.

SATURDAY 21ST JULY 2007

Playing their second game in 24 hours, Crystal Palace USA beat New Hampshire Phantoms 1-0 at Manchester Memorial HS thanks to an 89th minute winner from Sean Rush.

SATURDAY 21ST JULY 2001

A busy day in the pre-season for Crystal Palace as the first team faced Torquay United, the reserves took on Portsmouth and the under-17s and under-19s teams both played Brighton & Hove Albion at Beckenham.

FRIDAY 22ND JULY 2004

Crystal Palace completed the signing of Finnish international left-winger Joonas Kolkka on a three-year deal from Borussia Mönchengladbach. The flying Finn said: "It has always been a dream for me to play in the Premier League and when I got the chance I didn't have to think long about it."

FRIDAY 23RD JULY 2004

Iain Dowie bid £2.5 million for West Ham United player Michael Carrick and £1 million for team-mate Marlon Harewood. Southampton also received a bid of £1.5 million for Fitz Hall.

WEDNESDAY 23RD JULY 1997

Play-off hero David Hopkin departed for Premiership rivals Leeds United in a £3.5m deal.

SATURDAY 24TH JULY 2004

Crystal Palace travelled to Portman Road to face Ipswich Town in a less than prestigious pre-season friendly for both clubs! Just 5,282 turned up to watch the Tractor Boys win 2-1.

THURSDAY 25TH JULY 1991

Phil Barber moved to neighbours Millwall in a £100,000 deal after making 288 appearances for Crystal Palace.

SATURDAY 25TH JULY 1936

Left-handed opening Surrey batsman Laurie Fishlock, who made 19 appearances for Crystal Palace from 1929-1932, made his Test debut for England in the fixture against India at Old Trafford. Fishlock was bowled by Nayudu after making only six. The three-day match was eventually drawn.

TUESDAY 26TH JULY 1932

A tragic day in South London when Crystal Palace's brilliant young goalkeeper Billy Callender hung himself in one of the dressing rooms at Selhurst Park following the death of his beloved fiancée from polio. Callender played 225 senior matches for Palace, having moved to London as a 19-year-old from Northumberland.

TUESDAY 26TH JULY 1996

After weeks of speculation, Nigel Martyn became England's most expensive goalkeeper for the second time when he moved to join Howard Wilkinson at Leeds United for £2.5m.

SUNDAY 26TH JULY 1998

Crystal Palace crashed out of Europe at the first hurdle, going down 2-0 to Samsunspor in Turkey to lose 4-0 on aggregate in the Inter-Toto Cup. Werder Bremen of Germany or SK Lommel of Belgium would have been the next opponents en-route to a Uefa Cup spot.

FRIDAY 27TH JULY 1990

John Pemberton moved back up north when Crystal Palace accepted £300,000 for his services from Sheffield United. "Pembo" made 105 appearances for the Eagles.

SATURDAY 28TH JULY 2007

Crystal Palace USA set their highest-ever score record when they beat the hapless Bermuda Hogges 8-1 at the Navy-Marine Corps Stadium in Annapolis, Maryland.

SATURDAY 28TH JULY 2001

Robert Earnshaw scored a hat-trick for Cardiff City as Crystal Palace lost 4-0 at Ninian Park. It was Steve Bruce's first defeat as boss of the Eagles. The reserve team faced Hastings away in their pre-season campaign, whilst the academy under-17s played American side Temple Spirit at Beckenham.

SATURDAY 29TH JULY 1995

Crystal Palace treated Millwall as their feeder club once again when they snapped up Lions midfield star Andy Roberts for a club record fee of £2.5m. Ricky Newman also moved to The New Den as part of the deal. Sections of Roberts' Millwall supporting family refused to talk to Andy after he had made the move. David Hopkin also signed on this day for £750,000 from Chelsea.

SATURDAY 29TH JULY 2000

Crystal Palace continued their disastrous pre-season build-up when they lost 6-0 away to bitter rivals Millwall at The New Den. The match later proved to be Steve Coppell's final game in the Selhurst Park hot seat.

WEDNESDAY 30TH JULY 1969

Kumasi Asante Kotoko, one of Ghana's leading football clubs, visited Selhurst Park as part of their European tour. The Glaziers saw off the Porcupine Warriors 3-1.

TUESDAY 30TH JULY 2002

One legend left – and one in the making arrived – when Clinton Morrison moved from Crystal Palace in a big money, £4.25m transfer to Birmingham City whilst Andy Johnson turned up at Selhurst Park as a virtual makeweight in the deal. Morrison was reunited with his old manager Steve Bruce at Birmingham, who had guided the Midlands club to the Premiership thanks to victories against Millwall and then Norwich City in the play-offs.

WEDNESDAY 31ST JULY 1985

On trial from Greenwich Borough, Ian Wright was invited to turn out for the first team in their pre-season home friendly against Coventry City. Having caught the bus from his mum's house in Forest Hill to Crystal Palace Parade, Wright was wrongly directed to the athletics stadium rather than Selhurst Park. When he eventually turned up, Steve Coppell took him to one side and offered Wright a three-month contract paying £100 a week, which was eagerly accepted. The new Crystal Palace signing featured against the Sky Blues in a game that finished 1-1.

FRIDAY 31ST JULY 1998

The Eagles' Diary in the Crystal Palace programme reported a £2m double signing of, "two of the best young players in Argentina – 21-year-old Pablo Rodrigues and 19-year-old Cristian Ledesma". Apparently, the midfielders were, "being chased by the top clubs throughout Europe, but chose to become part of Terry Venables' and Mark Goldberg's big plans for Crystal Palace".

CRYSTAL PALACE
On This Day

AUGUST

FRIDAY 1st AUGUST 1997

Crystal Palace pulled off the biggest transfer in their history when they finally signed Italian international winger Attilio Lombardo from Juventus for £1.6m ahead of their 1997/98 season back in the Premiership. Lombardo arrived at Selhurst Park hoping to add to his vast collection of medals that included the Serie A title and Champions League with Juventus and the European Cup Winners' Cup, Serie A and Coppa Italia with Sampdoria. Ron Noades was so taken aback when he completed the signing that he was in no state to drive and so had to take a taxi home from Biggin Hill airport, the location where the Juventus delegation flew in and completed the signing of the deal.

TUESDAY 1st AUGUST 2000

The two most important men in Crystal Palace's recent history failed to get on and so Steve Coppell resigned the manager's job after clashing with new owner Simon Jordan following a string of heavy defeats in the pre-season warm-up campaign. "I didn't feel comfortable with Simon Jordan and neither did he with me," was how Coppell succinctly summed up the situation. Alan Smith returned to Selhurst Park from Fulham and filled the new vacancy, bringing with him from Craven Cottage Glenn Cockerill and Ray Houghton as coaches.

SATURDAY 2nd AUGUST 1997

Crystal Palace travelled to Gillingham to take on Brighton & Hove Albion in a pre-season friendly at their new temporary home ground, the Priestfield Stadium. Bruce Dyer saved the Eagles' blushes with a headed goal to make it 1-1 in what was nothing more than a fitness exercise in the sun. Jamie Fullerton and Hermann Hreidarsson were the new faces on show to the Palace fans.

TUESDAY 3rd AUGUST 1993

Crystal Palace journeyed down to the south coast to take on Brighton & Hove Albion in a pre-season friendly, and came away with a comfortable 3-0 win against the Seagulls.

MONDAY 4TH AUGUST 1997

Lombardo arrived at the Crystal Palace training ground down in Mitcham for the very first time. It was reported in the Palace match programme that his arrival caused quite a stir, with "several teammates guilty of lurking in corners, wide-eyed, watching the superstar eating a cheese roll". Ray Wilkins was also installed as a coach, his ability to converse in fluent Italian with Lombardo coming in handy.

SATURDAY 5TH AUGUST 2000

Alan Smith faced his old club Wycombe Wanderers for his first game back in charge at Crystal Palace, in what was his second spell in the managerial hot seat at Selhurst Park. As expected, the Adams Park crowd gave their former boss a hard time, and it was even worse on the pitch as Wycombe beat the Eagles 3-1 to cap a miserable pre-season campaign.

TUESDAY 6TH AUGUST 2002

Crystal Palace beat Crawley Town 4-0 at the Broadfield Stadium in a pre-season warm-up with Steve Kabba scoring all four. Officially a reserve team game, the Palace starting line-up read: Kolinko, Hunt, Frampton, Surey, Antwi, Berhalter, Routledge, Watson, Williams, Kabba, Rubins.

WEDNESDAY 6TH AUGUST 2008

Palace legend Clinton Morrison left his local club and moved to Coventry City, managed by Chris Coleman. The Eagles marksman's legacy was 113 goals to his name, which made him joint third highest goalscorer at Palace alongside Mark Bright.

MONDAY 7TH AUGUST 1995

Coventry City took John Salako to the West Midlands in a £1.5m transfer swoop, an offer that First Division Crystal Palace could not refuse.

SATURDAY 7TH AUGUST 1999

Heading into the first fixture of the 1999/00 season whilst still in administration, Crystal Palace faced Crewe Alexandra at Selhurst Park. Simon Rodger put Palace in front in the 67th minute after Lee Bradbury had missed a first-half penalty, but Steve Coppell's men were denied a win when substitute Mark Rivers slotted past Fraser Digby in the 84th minute.

THURSDAY 8TH AUGUST 1991

Steve Coppell raided Bradford City for their centre-half Lee Sinnott, the Bantams getting £350,000 for their man.

SATURDAY 8TH AUGUST 1998

Chas & Dave performed at Selhurst Park prior to the 2-2 draw with Bolton in the first home game of the First Division season. Palace Radio also aired for the first time.

SATURDAY 9TH AUGUST 1969

Crystal Palace played Manchester United in their first-ever top flight league fixture. The 48,610 crowd paid record receipts of £16,250 and packed into Selhurst to see Mel Blyth head Palace in front. Bobby Charlton levelled for United before Gerry Queen put the Glaziers back in front. Palace were denied an FAmous win when Willie Morgan pulled the Northerners level for a second time.

SATURDAY 9TH AUGUST 1997

A dream debut for Lombardo and a great start to the new Premiership season for Crystal Palace, as the Italian put the Eagles 1-0 up away at Everton. The former Juventus man then earned a penalty from which Bruce Dyer sent Palace 2-0 ahead before Duncan Ferguson scored a late consolation.

SATURDAY 9TH AUGUST 2003

Dougie Freedman plundered a hat-trick as Crystal Palace beat Burnley 3-2 on the opening day of the season, the club's first such three-goal haul since 1960 and the first-ever away from home.

SUNDAY 10TH AUGUST 1997

The Sunday papers linked Crystal Palace with everyone from Spurs striker Ronnie Rosenthal to Chelsea striker Gianluca Vialli.

SATURDAY 10TH AUGUST 1968

Midfielder Mel Blyth scored on his debut as Crystal Palace beat Cardiff City 4-0 in a Division Two encounter at Ninian Park. Blyth would represent Palace 262 times scoring 12 goals.

TUESDAY 11TH AUGUST 1998

Crystal Palace ventured to Devon to take on Torquay United in the first round, first leg of the Worthington Cup. The televised game saw Torquay take the lead, but Palace equalised through Attilio Lombardo who snaffled his first goal of the campaign.

TUESDAY 12TH AUGUST 1997

Palace took on Crawley in a friendly to mark the opening of their new Broadfield Stadium. Lombardo was on the scoresheet in a 5-0 win.

THURSDAY AUGUST 12TH 1999

With the club in administration, former owner Mark Goldberg resigned as chairman to be replaced by Peter Morley. Bizarrely, Goldberg then stepped up his efforts to own Palace once again as part of a City consortium that offered £16m for the Selhurst Park outfit.

WEDNESDAY 13TH AUGUST 1969

Crystal Palace sealed their first-ever top flight win in their second game in the First Division, when they beat Sunderland 2-0 at Selhurst Park thanks to strikes from Tony Taylor and Cliff Jackson.

SATURDAY 13TH AUGUST 1983

Kevin Mabbutt, the previous season's leading scorer, collided with Mick Mills of Southampton within minutes of a pre-season friendly and suffered a knee injury. It was a major blow for manager Alan Mullery, who lost his key striker for the bulk of the season.

THURSDAY 14TH AUGUST 1980

Terry Venables allowed Kenny Sansom to leave for Arsenal in an exchange deal that saw former QPR striker Clive Allen move to Selhurst Park, having spent only two months at Highbury and never once played a competitive game for the Gunners. Goalkeeper Paul Barron also made the switch from North to South London.

FRIDAY 14TH AUGUST 1998

Crystal Palace paraded their two Chinese signings to the media at the Streete Court training ground. Midfielder Fan Zhiyi was the national team captain, whilst Sun Jihai also represented his country.

SATURDAY 15TH AUGUST 1987

Steve Coppell gave full debuts to new signings Geoff Thomas, Neil Redfearn and home-grown talent John Salako in the season opener away to Huddersfield Town. Crystal Palace went two ahead thanks to Mark Bright, but the Terriers fought back to take a point.

WEDNESDAY 15TH AUGUST 1990

Centre-back Eric 'The Ninja' Young signed for Crystal Palace for £850,000 from Wimbledon, which provoked rumblings from those who thought that was excessive for a 30-year-old. Singapore-born Young, who represented Wales internationally, started his career at Slough Town before joining Brighton & Hove Albion, where he made 126 appearances in the league for the Seagulls, scoring 10 goals.

SATURDAY 15TH AUGUST 1992

The day football officially started if you were to believe Sky, as the Premier League made its bow and Crystal Palace became "founder members" of the new competition. Blackburn Rovers were first up at a scorching Selhurst Park, and all eyes were on Alan Shearer as he made his debut for the Lancashire club following his huge £3.6m transfer from Southampton. Palace had been in the hunt for the Newcastle-born forward the previous season to replace Ian Wright, but could not prise him away from the south coast. The match itself was a pulsating contest and ended 3-3. The honour of Palace's first Premier League goal went to Mark Bright who notched the opener. Shearer himself got a brace.

WEDNESDAY 15TH AUGUST 2001

Clinton Morrison made a goalscoring debut for the Republic of Ireland when he netted in the 2-2 friendly against Croatia at Lansdowne Road in Dublin.

THURSDAY 16TH AUGUST 1990

John Humphrey made a £450,000 switch from Charlton Athletic to Crystal Palace. The press took great pleasure in reporting that the former Addicks skipper didn't even need to move changing rooms as a result of his transfer, what with Charlton ground-sharing Selhurst Park with Palace.

MARK BRIGHT, STEVE COPPELL AND IAN WRIGHT

SATURDAY 17TH AUGUST 1968

Three games into the season, Crystal Palace led the Second Division following a superb 3-2 home win over Birmingham City.

WEDNESDAY 17TH AUGUST 1988

Swansea-born defender Jeff Hopkins arrived from Fulham for a tribunal-set fee of £240,000. Hopkins would play 70 times for Crystal Palace in the league, scoring twice, before moving to Bristol Rovers.

SUNDAY 18TH AUGUST 1985

Crystal Palace recorded their first opening-day success for four years when they beat their bogey team Shrewsbury Town at Gay Meadow 2-0, with Phil Barber and Andy Gray on target. The game was moved to the Sunday due to the annual flower show that occurred on the Saturday.

SATURDAY 18TH AUGUST 2001

Clinton Morrison scored twice in a routine 4-1 victory over Stockport County, his second strike was his 50th goal for Palace.

SATURDAY 19TH AUGUST 1972

Palace drew 1-1 in the league with eventual champions and Uefa Cup winners Liverpool at Selhurst Park but the match was marred when Peter Wall broke his leg in a tackle with former team-mate, Tommy Smith.

SATURDAY 19TH AUGUST 1967

Crystal Palace unveiled a new kit, the all-white one replaced with claret jerseys featuring thin light-blue stripes. The new attire was immediately successful as the Glaziers beat Rotherham United 3-0 at Millmoor on the opening day of the season.

SATURDAY 19TH AUGUST 1980

Vince Hilaire was sent off for pushing referee Alf Gray as Palace lost 4-3 in their first home game of the season to Tottenham Hotspur. A frustrating start to a miserable season was compounded as the 27,102 crowd was markedly down on the 45,583 that turned up for the last home game of the previous campaign, due to the 12,000 capacity Whitehorse Lane end being knocked down over the summer to make way for a supermarket and a new terrace that held just 5,000 fans.

SATURDAY 20TH AUGUST 1960

With Arthur Rowe now fully in charge, Crystal Palace adopted his famous "push and run" tactic that was so successful for him at Tottenham Hotspur. The move paid immediate dividends as the Glaziers beat Accrington Stanley 9-2 at Selhurst Park in their opening league fixture.

SATURDAY 20TH AUGUST 1955

Sir Stanley Rous, secretary of the FA, opened the new entrance hall and boardroom at Selhurst Park ahead of the opening game of the season against Northampton Town, which Crystal Palace lost 3-2.

THURSDAY 20TH AUGUST 1953

The season started on a Thursday evening due to England's participation in the 1954 World Cup in Switzerland, and Crystal Palace proceeded to draw 2-2 at home to Northampton Town. The earlier commencement of the league had an effect on the national team, as England progressed to the quarter-finals before being knocked out by Uruguay.

SATURDAY 20TH AUGUST 1949

Crystal Palace lost 2-1 away at Exeter City on the opening day of the season under yet another new manager, this time former Arsenal forward Ronnie Rooke who joined as player-manager. Guildford-born Rooke was something of a 'big name' in the game, having topped the scoring charts when helping Arsenal to the First Division title in 1947/48 with 33 league goals, a post-war season-best haul that not even Thierry Henry was able to beat. Employing Rooke, who had initially started out as a youngster at Palace in 1933 before moving to Fulham in 1936, was seen as a progressive appointment that would get the Glaziers promoted.

SATURDAY 21ST AUGUST 1948

The opening game of the 1948/49 season saw Crystal Palace revert to their original colours of claret and blue shirts and white shorts. The 'new' kit, which had not been worn for over a decade, did not help as the Glaziers crashed 5-1 at home to Reading.

SATURDAY 22ND AUGUST 1989

Not only were Manchester United the first visitors to Selhurst Park for the new First Division season, but the *Croydon Advertiser*-sponsored electronic scoreboard was switched on. Situated above the Whitehorse Lane terrace, it proudly displayed a 1-1 draw at the end of 90 minutes after Ian Wright rescued a point late on following Bryan Robson's 17th-minute opener.

SATURDAY 23RD AUGUST 1958

The inaugural Fourth Division season got off to a flyer for Crystal Palace as they thrashed Crewe Alexandra 6-2 at Selhurst Park in front of 13,551. Mike Deakin scored a first half hat-trick and 19-year-old Johnny Byrne then added three more.

SATURDAY 23RD AUGUST 1980

Clive Allen had his best game in Palace colours, scoring a hat-trick in the Eagles' 5-2 home win over Middlesbrough. But Palace did not win again in the league until mid October.

SATURDAY 24TH AUGUST 1963

Crystal Palace kicked-off what would be their most successful season in 39 years in awful fashion when then were hammered 5-1 away by Jimmy Hill's Coventry City.

SATURDAY 24TH AUGUST 1985

Micky Droy, having been persuaded to put off devoting time to his second-hand car business and re-sign for Crystal Palace for another year, sealed all three points for the Eagles as they beat Sunderland 1-0 at home in front of 7,040.

SATURDAY 24TH AUGUST 1996

The matchday programme for the Division One fixture against Oldham Athletic reported that Dave Bassett had sent Australian defender Tony Popovic home after playing twice for Crystal Palace in pre-season. "He wouldn't have added anything to the Palace squad," was Harry's assessment.

SATURDAY 25TH AUGUST 1945

Crystal Palace opened the new season with an unconvincing 0-0 draw at home to Aldershot. World War II may have been over in Europe at least, but it was still too early to revert back to the full peacetime fixture arrangements. Instead, the Football League divided the Third Division (South) teams into two sections, one for clubs situated north of the Thames, and one for those south.

SATURDAY 25TH AUGUST 1973

Inspired by Benfica, Palace began the season with a new nickname, 'Eagles', as Malcolm Allison sought a more assertive image for the club. Brighton & Hove Albion responded by replacing 'Dolphins' with 'Seagulls'.

SATURDAY 25TH AUGUST 1984

Steve Coppell entered into his first senior game in charge without captain Jim Cannon who had fractured his jaw in a pre-season friendly. Without the tough Glaswegian, the Eagles managed to draw 1-1 at home to Blackburn Rovers on the opening day of the season thanks to Stan Cummins. Even with a new manager, the crowd was still a woeful 6,764.

SATURDAY 25TH AUGUST 1990

A large number of Crystal Palace fans managed to get past Luton Town's ban on away fans to witness Eric Young score on his debut after just 15 minutes to put the Eagles in the lead. But the Hatters pulled one back on the stroke of half-time and Coppell's men had to leave the plastic pitch of Kenilworth Road with a point on the opening day of the season.

SATURDAY 26TH AUGUST 1933

Manager Jack Tresadern declared that, "It is going to be Palace's year," ahead of the opening fixture that saw Crystal Palace triumph 4-0 away to Southend. It was an FAlse dawn as the Glaziers finished in mid-table.

SATURDAY 26TH AUGUST 1995

Ron Noades and Steve Coppell officially opened the new Holmesdale Road stand when they cut the ribbon before the second home game of the season against Charlton Athletic. Double-tiered, and with a capacity of 8,500, it cost the club nearly £6m which was financed by a mixture of bank loans, grants from the Football Trust and long-term season ticket sales.

SATURDAY 27TH AUGUST 1921

Crystal Palace faced the mighty Nottingham Forest at The Nest in their first-ever fixture in the Second Division. Forest handed a debut to England international goalkeeper Sam Hardy but it couldn't stop the league's newcomers romping to a 4-1 win in front of 20,000. Welsh international centre-half JT Jones had the distinction of scoring Palace's first-ever goal in the second tier of English football following a 25th minute header.

SATURDAY 27TH AUGUST 1983

Red and blue stripes were back for the adidas-manufactured home kit, as Crystal Palace started the season with their first-ever shirt sponsor in the form of Red Rose. But the new strip didn't affect Manchester City as they won 2-0 at Selhurst Park.

SATURDAY 27TH AUGUST 1988

Crystal Palace were due to start what would be their glorious 1988/89 promotion season, but instead had to sit out their first fixture, away to Swindon Town, as the Wiltshire outfit were behind with their ground improvement work.

FRIDAY 27TH AUGUST 1999

Goalkeeper Kevin Miller was offloaded to Barnsley for £250,000 after he refused to play for Crystal Palace after his wages were delayed due to the club being in administration.

WEDNESDAY 28TH AUGUST 1957

Crystal Palace lost their first home league game of the season, going down 1-0 to Millwall. The new national Fourth Division was introduced the following season, so the Glaziers were aiming to finish 11th or better to avoid dropping out of third tier of English football.

SATURDAY 28TH AUGUST 1920

Palace's first-ever Football League fixture, in the newly-formed Third Division, ended in disappointment with a 2-1 reverse away to Merthyr Town at Pennydarren Park.

SATURDAY 28TH AUGUST 1982

Alan Mullery's first game in charge of Crystal Palace drew just 7,549 to Selhurst Park for the opening game of the season against Barnsley. Vince Hilaire scored in the 1-1 draw.

TUESDAY 28TH AUGUST 1990

The Arthur Wait stand was all-seated when Chelsea were the first visitors to Selhurst Park at the start of the glorious 1990/91 season, a campaign when Crystal Palace were never out of the top five of the First Division. Andy Gray scored from the spot in the fifth minute but was sent off soon after with Dennis Wise following a brawl, leaving it for Ian Wright to get the decisive strike for a 2-1 win in front of 27,101 fans.

SATURDAY 29TH AUGUST 1925

Crystal Palace lost their opening game of the season 2-1 at home to Millwall. Tipton-born midfielder Billy 'Rubber' Turner, signed from Bromsgrove in the summer, featured for Palace and would go on to make 302 appearances scoring 37 goals in the process.

SATURDAY 29TH AUGUST 1981

Crystal Palace were awarded a penalty after just 55 seconds in the opening game of the season against Cambridge United at Selhurst Park. Paul Hinshelwood tucked it away, and was also on target again before the break as the Eagles were awarded a second spot kick. The third penalty of the game went to the Us in the second half, which they converted, and the final score was 2-1 to Dario Gradi's men in front of just 11,201. In West London, Palace reserves played their first competitive match on plastic as they took on QPR's second string on the artificial surface at Loftus Road.

SATURDAY 30TH AUGUST 1941

Crystal Palace, along with all London clubs plus Aldershot, Brighton & Hove Albion, Reading and Watford, kicked-off the new wartime season in a breakaway competition following a disagreement with the Football League over their plans. A 2-0 win at Selhurst Park against Millwall got Palace's London League campaign off to the best possible start.

SATURDAY 30TH AUGUST 1924

More than 25,000 turned up to watch Crystal Palace play their first game at their new home, Selhurst Park. The Wednesday, having not yet adopted the prefix of 'Sheffield', provided the opposition and their international packed team won 1-0, having taken the lead after just four minutes. Sir Louis Newton, Lord Mayor of London, officially opened the new stadium which at the time consisted of just the Main Stand complemented by grassy banks. Humphrey's of Knightsbridge had the £30,000 contract to complete the ground but an industrial dispute meant that not all of the seats were installed in time for the visit of The Wednesday.

SATURDAY 30TH AUGUST 1924

As Crystal Palace started the new season at Selhurst Park, The Nest was sublet to local side Tramway FC. Under the lease terms, Tramway paid Palace all expenses and 10% of their gross gate. But The Nest didn't last long, as over the next few years the Selhurst Rail Depot was built on the site.

TUESDAY 30TH AUGUST 1988

Crystal Palace started their promotion season on a Tuesday night with a 1-1 draw at home to Chelsea, courtesy of a Neil Redfearn effort, in front of 17,490 at Selhurst Park.

SATURDAY 31ST AUGUST 1918

Millwall were the first visitors to The Nest, playing Crystal Palace in a friendly in aid of Croydon Hospitals. The Mayor of Croydon, Alderman Howard Houlder, welcomed the sides and kicked off. Palace eventually won 4-1 after Millwall had taken the lead.

SATURDAY 31ST AUGUST 2002

Crystal Palace ventured up to Turf Moor to face Burnley, managed by ex-Eagles coach Stan Ternent. The game was a dour affair, ending 0-0, with neither side carving out many clear-cut chances. It was Trevor Francis' second 0-0 draw in a row, but his team would make up for this when they hammered Wolverhampton Wanderers 4-2 in their next league game. The 17-year-old Wayne Routledge scored after just a minute on his full debut.

CRYSTAL PALACE
On This Day

SEPTEMBER

TUESDAY 1st SEPTEMBER 1992

Steve Coppell paid neighbours Millwall £1m for their highly-rated striker Chris Armstrong.

SATURDAY 1st SEPTEMBER 2001

Aki Riihilahti played in a 2-0 win over Albania in Tirana, as Finland attempted to qualify for the 2002 World Cup.

SATURDAY 2nd SEPTEMBER 1939

Crystal Palace played their final league game of the 1939/1940 season when they beat Bristol Rovers 3-0 at Selhurst Park. The next day war was declared against Nazi Germany, which forced the Football League to be annulled and players' contracts to be suspended.

SATURDAY 2nd SEPTEMBER 1995

Dean Gordon became Crystal Palace's most capped under-21 player when he made his 12th appearance for England in a European Championship qualifier away to Portugal. Just 1,500 people were in Oporto as England lost 2-0.

THURSDAY 3rd SEPTEMBER 1970

Gareth Southgate was born in Watford, and besides making 191 appearances for Crystal Palace and scoring 22 goals in the process, Southgate also earned a total of 57 caps for England during his career.

SATURDAY 3rd SEPTEMBER 2005

Finland embarrassingly drew 0-0 away at Andorra in a World Cup qualifier in which Crystal Palace midfielder Aki Riihilahti was involved.

WEDNESDAY 4th SEPTEMBER 1963

Edmonton-born Bobby Kellard signed for Crystal Palace from Southend United. The 5ft 6in tall midfielder made 137 appearances at Selhurst Park over two spells, scoring 10 goals.

THURSDAY 4th DECEMBER 1986

Richard Shaw signed professional forms for Crystal Palace. The Park Royal-born defender had already won the club's Young Player of the Year award for 1986, under the guidance of youth boss Alan Smith.

WEDNESDAY 5TH SEPTEMBER 1956

Crystal Palace played their first league match under floodlights when they took on Reading at Selhurst Park, drawing 1-1. Prior to the start of the 1955/56 season, the Football League changed its policy and agreed to allow matches under it's control to take place under artificial light but only if both sides were in agreement.

SATURDAY 5TH SEPTEMBER 1998

Palace had two internationals playing in European Championship qualifiers, David Amsalem for Israel and Hermann Hreidarsson for Iceland.

SATURDAY 6TH SEPTEMBER 1980

Clive Allen smashed a free-kick that rebounded from the stanchion *inside* the net but the goal was disallowed, as the referee thought the ball had bounced off the crossbar instead. Crystal Palace then lost the Division One fixture against Coventry City at Highfield Road 3-1.

WEDNESDAY 6TH SEPTEMBER 2006

Shefki Kuqi came on as a second-half substitute for Roy Hodgson's Finland as they took a credible 1-1 draw in their European Championships qualifier against Portugal in Helsinki.

WEDNESDAY 7TH SEPTEMBER 1966

Crystal Palace headed up to Molineux to face Wolverhampton Wanderers, the team line-ups having David Burnside listed to play for the Glaziers. But Burnside was sold to the Black Country club on the day and actually scored for Wolves in a 1-1 draw.

SATURDAY 7TH SEPTEMBER 1985

Crystal Palace lost 3-1 at The Valley in a game of four penalties, but the really significant news of the afternoon was the announcement that Charlton Athletic would leave their home and ground-share at Selhurst Park with Palace the following month.

FRIDAY 7TH SEPTEMBER 2007

Matt Lawrence scored his first goal for the Eagles, heading home Danny Butterfield's 28th minute corner, as Crystal Palace beat Crystal Palace USA in a mid-season friendly at Selhurst Park.

FRIDAY 8TH SEPTEMBER 1995

Popular striker Iain Dowie was lured back to the Premiership courtesy of West Ham United who coughed up £500,000. The Hatfield-born forward played 25 times for the Eagles, scoring 10 goals.

FRIDAY 8TH SEPTEMBER 1995

A special day in the history of Crystal Palace when Ray Lewington finally got his man and brought Dougie Freedman to Selhurst Park, having wanted to take the Glaswegian striker with him to Fulham two years earlier. Crystal Palace gave Barnet £800,000 for the future Palace legend.

TUESDAY 9TH SEPTEMBER 1997

Bruce Dyer was man of the match when he starred in England under-21s' 1-0 victory over Moldova. A crowd of 5,534 were present at Adams Park, Wycombe for the European Championship qualifier.

SATURDAY 9TH SEPTEMBER 2006

£2.5m signing Shefki Kuqi failed to impress on his debut as Crystal Palace lost 2-1 away at Luton in the Championship. It left Peter Taylor without a win in four games.

WEDNESDAY 10TH SEPTEMBER 1997

Ron Noades revealed that Crystal Palace put in a £6.5m bid for Lazio's Giuseppe Signori, only for the Rome club to offer the 29-year-old a new contract which he then signed, scuppering any move.

SATURDAY 10TH SEPTEMBER 2005

Clinton Morrison started his first game at Selhurst Park following his £2m transfer from Birmingham City and marked it with the opening goal of the game, whilst Andy Johnson grabbed his fifth of the season as Crystal Palace beat Hull City 2-0 in the league.

SATURDAY 11TH SEPTEMBER 1999

Despite Clinton Morrison opening the scoring, Crystal Palace lost 2-1 to Manchester City in front of 31,541 at Maine Road. The result plunged the Eagles to the bottom of Division One, their lowest ranking for 15 years.

TUESDAY 11TH SEPTEMBER 1990

Eric Young won his second Welsh cap, and first as a Crystal Palace player, when Terry Yorath started him alongside the likes of Ian Rush and Mark Hughes in a friendly against Denmark in Copenhagen.

WEDNESDAY 11TH SEPTEMBER 1991

Crystal Palace's John Salako made his last appearance for England, when he lined up alongside Gary Lineker and Alan Smith for the friendly against Germany at Wembley. Karl-Heinz Riedle won the game for the visitors 1-0, and Salako was replaced by Paul Stewart in the 67th minute.

WEDNESDAY 12TH SEPTEMBER 1962

After a club record twenty consecutive league games without a victory, Crystal Palace finally managed to take maximum points when they beat QPR 1-0 at Selhurst Park.

TUESDAY 12TH SEPTEMBER 1989

Geoff Thomas put the ball on the penalty spot in front of the Kop at Anfield as Crystal Palace assistant manager Stan Ternent turned to Steve Coppell and said: "If he scores this penalty we're running on". Coppell agreed to the two man pitch invasion, but the Palace captain blasted the ball into row Z and the two men slumped back into the dugout. The Eagles were already 6-0 down and eventually lost an ultimately meaningless league game against the eventual champions 9-0.

WEDNESDAY 12TH SEPTEMBER 2001

Championship side Crystal Palace travelled up to Goodison Park in the second round of the League Cup and claimed yet another Premiership scalp when they beat Everton 5-4 on penalties after the match had finished one apiece. Duncan Ferguson was on target first for Walter Smith's men, scoring from the spot in the sixth minute, whilst Dougie Freedman grabbed his 50th Palace goal when he equalised, also from the spot in the 10th minute.

TUESDAY 13TH SEPTEMBER 1980

Crystal Palace lost 2-1 at home to Ipswich Town in front of 24,283 and dropped to the bottom of Division One.

SATURDAY 13TH SEPTEMBER 1997

Crystal Palace slumped to a 3-0 defeat at the hands of Ruud Gullit's Chelsea in what was an easy win for the West Londoners. Mark Hughes opened the scoring after just 20 minutes before a Frank Leboeuf penalty six minutes later doubled the advantage. Graeme Le Saux rubbed salt into the wounds by adding a third right at the death.

SATURDAY 14TH SEPTEMBER 1940

Thirty minutes into the South Regional League fixture against Millwall at The Den, play was halted due to an air-raid warning siren. Wartime football rules stated that no matter how early a game was stopped, the result would still stand. The Lions were 1-0 up at the time and so were handed a quick victory over Crystal Palace.

SATURDAY 14TH SEPTEMBER 1929

Manager Fred Mavin gave Peter Simpson his league debut when Norwich City were the visitors to Selhurst Park. Simpson made an immediate impact and scored a hat-trick on his debut which helped his new team to a 3-2 victory. Simpson scored a club record 36 goals that season.

SATURDAY 14TH SEPTEMBER 1918

QPR were the first league visitors to Crystal Palace's new ground The Nest, located opposite Selhurst station, and were handsomely beaten 4-2. The Nest had previously been used by local rivals Croydon Common but they went bust in February 1917. The owners of the stadium, The London Brighton & South Coast Railway Company, were more than happy when Palace took on the lease. The Ecclesiastical Commissioners for England actually owned the land the stadium was on, which explained why the lease stipulated that football could not be played at The Nest on Good Friday or Christmas Day. In the 1918/19 season, Palace's home fixture against Arsenal fell on Good Friday and had to be played at Millwall.

WEDNESDAY 14TH SEPTEMBER 1983

A low point for Crystal Palace under Alan Mullery, as the Eagles surrendered a 3-0 lead from the first leg away at Peterborough United in the League Cup. The Fourth Division side levelled the tie on aggregate thanks to a 3-0 victory after extra time at Selhurst Park. The Posh then won 4-2 on penalties to progress to the second round.

SATURDAY 15TH SEPTEMBER 1984

Steve Coppell's first encounter with the old foe Brighton & Hove Albion didn't go well as Albion beat Crystal Palace 1-0 at the Goldstone, leaving the Eagles bottom of the Second Division.

SATURDAY 16TH SEPTEMBER 1978

Crystal Palace beat Millwall 3-0 at The Den as Kenny Sansom made his 100th league appearance.

SATURDAY 17TH SEPTEMBER 2005

Crystal Palace lost 1-0 in the Championship against Cardiff City at Ninian Park following England one-cap wonder Michael Ricketts' 26th minute strike.

MONDAY 17TH SEPTEMBER 1984

Terry Byfield, the longest-serving of any of the current crop of staff at Crystal Palace, joined the club. Starting out on the Youth Training Scheme as a receptionist, Byfield helped set up the publications department with Pete King before being made the Assistant Club Secretary to Mike Hurst. A return to the Communications Department at Selhurst Park followed.

WEDNESDAY 18TH SEPTEMBER 1974

Terry Venables and Ian Evans made their debuts as Crystal Palace lost 2-0 away to Hereford. The duo joined from QPR in the deal that saw Don Rogers go the other way.

TUESDAY 18TH SEPTEMBER 2001

Strikes from Jovan Kirovski, Dougie Freedman, Clinton Morrison and centre-back Tony Popovic, who contributed headed goals, fired Steve Bruce's Crystal Palace to a 5-0 win over Grimsby in Division One. A 13,970 crowd were at Selhurst to witness the rout.

SATURDAY 19TH SEPTEMBER 1908

Charlie McGibbon became the first Crystal Palace striker to net a hat-trick on their debut, as he inspired Palace to a 4-0 home win over Brighton & Hove Albion.

SATURDAY 19TH SEPTEMBER 1992

Chris Armstrong made it four goals in two games as Crystal Palace beat Everton 2-0 at Goodison Park in front of 18,080. The win was the Eagles first ever victory in the Premier League.

SATURDAY 20TH SEPTEMBER 1913

Shepherds Bush-born Ben Bateman made his debut for Crystal Palace in the home game against Exeter City in the Southern League. At the time, most of the club's players came from the north or the Midlands so the fans took Londoner Bateman to their hearts. The outside-right represented England at amateur international level and scored 11 goals in 180 appearances for the Glaziers.

SATURDAY 20TH SEPTEMBER 1997

An 80th-minute winner from Attilio Lombardo settled a dour 'away' meeting with Wimbledon in front of 16,747 at Selhurst Park.

SATURDAY 21ST SEPTEMBER 1991

Crystal Palace recorded their fourth win of the season in the First Division with a 3-2 victory over Oldham Athletic at Boundary Park in front of 13,391 fans. Mark Bright grabbed the winner following strikes from John Salako and Ian Wright. It was Wright's last appearance for the Eagles as by the Monday he had signed for Arsenal, having played 277 times for Palace and scored 117 goals.

SATURDAY 21ST SEPTEMBER 1996

David Tuttle, Dougie Freedman, Kevin Muscat, Bruce Dyer (pen), Carl Veat and George Ndah were all on target as Crystal Palace smashed Reading 6-1 in the league at Elm Park.

SATURDAY 22ND SEPTEMBER 1990

High-flying Palace made the short trip to White Hart Lane to face Terry Venables' star-studded Tottenham Hotspur team in a highly-anticipated Division One encounter. A full house of 34,859 watched as Paul Gascoigne, fresh from his Italia 90 World Cup exploits, fired Spurs into the lead just before the break with a sweetly struck free-kick. But after the interval it was one-way traffic from Palace and a point was secured when Geoff Thomas slid home Mark Bright's neat square pass ten minutes from time.

SATURDAY 22ND SEPTEMBER 2001

Aki Riihilahti fired a last-minute winner to ensure Crystal Palace collected all three points in a drab league encounter with Barnsley at Selhurst Park. Manager Steve Bruce had loan signing Steve Vickers in the side and his presence helped the Eagles look a bit more solid defensively, but there was to be no repeat of the 5-0 annihilation that Grimsby Town suffered four days earlier for the 15,433 crowd.

SATURDAY 23RD SEPTEMBER 1939

Crystal Palace played their first game after the outbreak of World War II and the annulment of the Football League, when they visited Guildford City for a friendly. The Southern League side humiliated Palace 5-0.

MONDAY 23RD SEPTEMBER 1991

Arsenal smashed their transfer fee record by £1.2m when they paid Crystal Palace £2.5m for star striker Ian Wright. The Gunners made their move after learning of a clause in Wright's contract that would allow him to move to a club that could offer him European football. Wright himself had been getting itchy feet since Palace hadn't signed the calibre of players he had hoped for during the summer and was spoiling for a move to a club where he could win "everything". Ironically, Tottenham Hotspur had also shown some interest in Wright. Chairman Ron Noades hailed the offer as "too good for Palace and for Wright to refuse".

TUESDAY 24TH SEPTEMBER 1991

The *Daily Mirror* suggested that Ron Noades was about to blow £3m on Wimbledon's John Fashanu to replace the recently departed Ian Wright or failing that, make a move for Cambridge United's Dion Dublin. The paper also carried a picture exclusive of Wright posing in Arsenal's yellow 'bruised banana' away kit.

WEDNESDAY 24TH SEPTEMBER 1997

Jamie Fullarton scored his first goal for Crystal Palace in a 1-1 draw away to Coventry City in the Premiership. Dougie Freedman also made his 100th appearance for the Eagles before being replaced by goal-machine Carl Veart in the 79th minute.

SATURDAY 25TH SEPTEMBER 1954

A dour 0-0 draw at home to Swindon Town was the final straw for the Crystal Palace board of directors who decided to relieve manager Laurie Scott of his post, following a disastrous start of just six points from the opening ten matches.

TUESDAY 25TH SEPTEMBER 1990

A memorable night at Selhurst Park as Crystal Palace thumped Southend United 8-0 in the first leg of a second round Rumbelow's Cup tie. Mark Bright and Ian Wright both wanted the match ball as they scored a hat-trick apiece, whilst Glyn Hodges and Garry Thompson also got themselves on the scoresheet. It was Palace's biggest ever victory in any cup competition.

SATURDAY 26TH SEPTEMBER 1942

Another wartime league fixture against Brighton & Hove Albion: and another huge victory. Crystal Palace thumped their south-coast rivals 8-1 on their way to a lowly 15th-place finish in the Wartime Football League South.

SATURDAY 26TH SEPTEMBER 1981

Dario Gradi complained of "woeful finishing" as a sorry Crystal Palace were beaten 1-0 by Shrewsbury Town to drop into the bottom third of the Second Division. Fans voted with their feet as just 9,037 bothered to turn up at Selhurst Park.

TUESDAY 27TH SEPTEMBER 1983

A month into the Second Division campaign and already in the relegation places, Crystal Palace finally recorded their first victory of the season under the floodlights at Selhurst against Portsmouth. It took a Mark Hateley own goal to be the difference as Alan Mullery's men won 2-1 in front of 8,486 fans.

WEDNESDAY 27TH SEPTEMBER 1995

Bristol Rovers were laughing all the way to the bank as Crystal Palace paid a staggering £1.25m fee for striker Gareth Taylor.

SUNDAY 27TH SEPTEMBER 1998

Fan Zhiyi made his home debut for Crystal Palace in a 1-0 win over Sheffield United in the First Division. The match was beamed live to China where a TV audience of 500 million got to see some great play from Lombardo as well as Sasa Curcic hitting the only goal of the game in the 74th minute. China also saw Walter Del Rio come on as an 86th minute substitute for the Eagles, alongside Gareth Taylor missing an easy chance for the Blades.

MONDAY 28TH SEPTEMBER 1953

Selhurst Park's first-ever set of floodlights were officially opened by chairman David Harris ahead of a friendly against Chelsea. The spirited Glaziers grabbed a 1-1 draw against their top-flight opponents in front of 17,082.

SATURDAY 28TH SEPTEMBER 1991

Stan Collymore scored his one and only league goal for Crystal Palace in a 2-2 away draw against QPR in the top flight. Mark Bright was Palace's other scorer.

SATURDAY 29TH SEPTEMBER 1945

Standards slipped at Selhurst Park as Crystal Palace only beat Brighton & Hove Albion 5-1 in the last wartime league season.

SATURDAY 29TH SEPTEMBER 1979

For the first time in their history, Crystal Palace were the best team in the land when they sat at the top of the First Division thanks to an irresistible 4-1 thumping of Bobby Robson's Ipswich Town at Selhurst Park. Dave Swindlehurst, Paul Hinshelwood and Gerry Francis had the Eagles 3-0 up before Town pulled one back before the break. Jim Cannon's volley in the second half was the sweetest strike, as it capped a wonderful move and was also the goal that Palace needed to head the league on goal difference from Manchester United and Nottingham Forest.

WEDNESDAY 30TH SEPTEMBER 1908

Crystal Palace ended the month having had their first-ever player sent off, when Jimmy Bauchop was dismissed in a London Cup fixture against local rivals Croydon Common.

SATURDAY 30TH SEPTEMBER 1967

A bumper crowd of 38,006 packed into Selhurst to see Crystal Palace beat QPR 1-0 and in the process go top of the Second Division for the first time in their history. Terry Long was the match-winner, pouncing in the 39th minute.

SATURDAY 30TH SEPTEMBER 1939

Due to the outbreak of World War II, the Football League announced regional competitions would take the place of the national leagues. Third Division (South) Crystal Palace found themselves in with the First Division London teams as well as Watford, Southend and Norwich City in the Football League South 'A' Division.

FRIDAY 30TH SEPTEMBER 1910

Crystal Palace captain George Woodger completed a move to First Division Oldham Athletic, for a fee reported to be "up to £800", in order to achieve his aim of gaining international recognition. The classy centre-forward fulfilled his ambition, winning his one and only England cap in their 2-1 win over Ireland in February 1911 at the Baseball Ground, Derby.

SATURDAY 30TH SEPTEMBER 1995

Dougie Freedman scored his first goal for Palace in the 1-1 league draw with Stoke City. A Selhurst crowd of 14,613 saw a legend born.

CRYSTAL PALACE
On This Day

OCTOBER

SATURDAY 1st OCTOBER 1938

Ahead of the 4-2 home victory over Clapton Orient, Crystal Palace chairman Mr E T Truett called for three cheers from the crowd for Prime Minister Neville Chamberlain after his return from Nazi Germany the day before declaring "Peace For Our Time".

SATURDAY 1st OCTOBER 1949

Full-back Fred Dawes, the only Crystal Palace player to complete a century of appearances either side of World War II, suffered a head injury in the 2-0 defeat away to Bournemouth that signalled the end of his illustrious playing career.

SATURDAY 1st OCTOBER 1977

Crystal Palace lost 3-2 at home to Fulham but the day was marred when club captain and defender Ian Evans broke his leg in a tackle with George Best. Evans was unable to play again for two years.

TUESDAY 1st OCTOBER 1991

Palace faced Leeds United in a First Division fixture that was meant to be played at the start of the season, but owing to ground improvements to Selhurst Park not being completed in time, the game was postponed. Marco Gabbiadini, a £1.8m capture from Sunderland to replace Ian Wright, made his debut but it was Mark Bright who won the game when he scored the only goal.

SATURDAY 1st OCTOBER 1994

Crystal Palace recorded their first-ever league victory at Highbury, and their first win of the season, when John Salako's brace condemned George Graham's men to their fourth defeat of the campaign. Ian Wright scored his 100th goal for Arsenal with a 72nd minute header but it was only a consolation in a game where the former Palace favourite was booked for throwing the ball at George Ndah.

WEDNESDAY 2nd OCTOBER 1991

After falling badly in the previous night's fixture against Leeds, John Salako had an exploratory operation that revealed the severance of both cruciate ligaments behind his left knee. It was a terrible injury and saw Salako out of action for months.

SATURDAY 2ND OCTOBER 1993

John Salako started for the first time after two years out through injury, and made an instant impact when he scored a hat-trick against visiting Stoke City in a Division One fixture at Selhurst Park. Crystal Palace won 4-1, Gareth Southgate opened the scoring for Alan Smith's men, and the result sent the Eagles top of the table.

TUESDAY 3RD OCTOBER 1995

Leon McKenzie scored the second goal in a 2-0 win over Southend United in the second leg of a second round League Cup tie at Selhurst Park. At just 17 years, 139 days old Croydon-born McKenzie – son of British boxing champion Clinton McKenzie and nephew of World boxing champion Duke McKenzie – entered the history books as the youngest Crystal Palace player to score on their senior debut.

SATURDAY 3RD OCTOBER 1998

Crystal Palace's starting line-up away at Ipswich Town in Division One was a real league of nations with China (Zhiyi), Australia (Foster and Rizzo), Italy (Lombardo), Yugoslavia (Curcic), Sweden (Svensson) and, of course, England (Digby, Burton, Tuttle, Warhurst and Mullins) all represented. Scottish midfielder Steven Thomson turned out as a sub, whilst Argentinian midfielder Walter Del Rio remained on the bench. But, the cosmopolitan mix didn't help as Terry Venables watched his men try to play a short passing game but they failed to make headway against a resolute Ipswich defence and eventually lost 3-0.

SATURDAY 4TH OCTOBER 1930

Peter Simpson became the first and only Crystal Palace player to score six goals in a league fixture, inspiring the Glaziers to a 7-2 demolition of Exeter City in front of 12,805 at Selhurst Park.

SATURDAY 4TH OCTOBER 1986

Crystal Palace went top of the Second Division for the first time since May 1979 in the sweetest way possible after coming from behind to beat Millwall 2-1 at Selhurst Park, thanks to second-half strikes from former Lion Anton Otulakowski and Tony Finnigan.

THURSDAY 5TH OCTOBER 2000

International weekend loomed and the key fixture was Kevin Keegan's England versus Germany at the 'old' Wembley. Palace flew out for a four-day training camp near Seville in Spain where the facilities came very highly recommended, as Manchester United would use them in January.

SATURDAY 5TH OCTOBER 2002

Dele Adebola put Crystal Palace ahead in the 77th minute away at Stoke City, as Andy Johnson made his return following injury. But Chris Iwelumo levelled for the home side in the 85th minute and denied the Eagles their first win in five league matches. Nikolaos Michopoulos started in goal for Trevor Francis' men, having been bought in on loan from Burnley following injuries to both Matt Clarke and Alex Kolinko.

TUESDAY 6TH OCTOBER 1953

Crystal Palace organised a second successive game against top-flight opposition in order to celebrate the installation of floodlights at Selhurst Park, and to help pay for them! Cardiff City played their part in a 2-2 draw, and combined with the gate receipts from this match and the previous floodlit friendly against Chelsea, Palace were left with their new lighting paid for *and* a £1,400 profit.

SUNDAY 6TH OCTOBER 1996

After a day of talks with Ron Noades and Francis Lee of Manchester City, Steve Coppell faxed Lee at 4pm to accept the position of manager at Maine Road. But Coppell lasted just six games in charge, and left the role after 33 days citing the pressures of the job: "I'm not ashamed to admit that I have suffered for some time from huge pressure I have imposed upon myself, and since my appointment this has completely overwhelmed me to such an extent that I cannot function in the job the way I would like to. As this situation is affecting my well-being, I have asked Francis Lee to relieve me of my obligation to manage the club on medical advice."

SATURDAY 6TH OCTOBER 2001

Dougie Freedman finally made his debut for Scotland, starting in the World Cup qualifier at Hampden against Latvia, who featured club teammates Aleksandrs Kolinko in goal and Andrejs Rubins in attack. Craig Brown's Scotland could still have qualified for Korea/Japan 2002 if they had scored a stack-load against Latvia and Belgium had beaten Croatia in Zagreb, but as it was Scotland had to come from behind to grab a 2-1 win after Rubins had put the visitors in front. Freedman then equalised for the Scots, his effort going in off Rubins, before David Weir won the match sending the sparse crowd of 23,228 home with at least a win to cheer, if not qualification.

SATURDAY 7TH OCTOBER 2000

Alex Kolinko earned the first of the 20 caps for Latvia as a Palace player, as he let in four in a World Cup qualifier against Belgium in Riga.

SUNDAY 7TH OCTOBER 2001

Fan Zhiyi started for China as they beat Oman 1-0 in a World Cup qualifier at the Wulihe Stadium in Shenyang. Eight days later Fan moved to Dundee for £300,000

SATURDAY 7TH OCTOBER 2006

Gabor Kiraly played for Hungary as they lost 1-0 at home to Turkey in a European Championship qualifier. It was Kiraly's penultimate international cap as a Crystal Palace player.

WEDNESDAY 8TH OCTOBER 1980

Terry Venables was linked with QPR, but Crystal Palace chairman Ray Bloye stated: "He has just signed a contract with us".

SATURDAY 8TH OCTOBER 1988

Crystal Palace put four past Blackburn Rovers at Ewood Park, but still lost 5-4, in the rain. Steve Coppell referred to the result as "really smelly".

MONDAY 8TH OCTOBER 2007

After drawing 1-1 away to his old club Hull City, Peter Taylor had his contract as manager of Crystal Palace terminated following a mediocre spell in charge from the former Eagles legend.

WEDNESDAY 9TH OCTOBER 1996

Dougie Freedman made the bench for Scotland's World Cup qualifier against Estonia in the Kadriorg Stadium in Tallinn. However, when the game was switched from a 6.45pm kick-off to a 3pm start on the morning of the game due to the inadequate floodlights, the hosts refused to show, ludicrously stating that not enough notice was given. Craig Brown's Scotland kicked-off against no opposition and referee Miroslav Radoman had no choice but to abandon the game after just three seconds, denying Freedman a chance to get on as a substitute and win his first cap.

SATURDAY 9TH OCTOBER 2004

Gabor Kiraly and Sandor Torghelle both played for Hungary as they lost 3-0 to Sweden in a World Cup qualifier. On the same night, Crystal Palace had further international representation when Joonas Kolkka and Aki Riihilahti both played for Finland against Armenia, winning 3-1.

SATURDAY 10TH OCTOBER 1959

Crystal Palace recorded their biggest ever league victory when they absolutely hammered the hapless Barrow 9-0 in front of 9,500 at Selhurst Park. Left winger Ray Colfar opened the scoring, followed by Johnny Gavin who netted direct from a corner. Roy Summersby then scored a brace before half-time which sent Palace in 4-0 at the break. Soon after the restart, Colfar hit his second. Summersby then got his hat-trick, soon followed by his fourth from the penalty spot after a handball just after the hour. Johnny Byrne had an effort disallowed before scoring two as the match ended.

SATURDAY 10TH OCTOBER 1970

Crystal Palace travelled to Old Trafford to face Manchester United in a league fixture given an added twist due to the fact that it was Bobby Charlton's 500th league appearance for the Reds. Palace hadn't read the script and secured an impressive 1-0 victory that spoilt Charlton's day thanks to Bobby Tambling's effort from the edge of the penalty area just after the hour.

DOUGIE FREEDMAN

SATURDAY 10TH OCTOBER 1987

The very first issue of *Eagle Eye* was sold outside Selhurst Park ahead of the Division Two clash with Millwall, which Crystal Palace went on to win 1-0. The fanzine was one of the most influential publications of its type with even Ron Noades known to flick through its pages from time to time, probably having raised a wry smile at features that told fans how they could make a Brighton top from a Tesco's carrier bag. Noades probably didn't find the "incorporating the *Palace Echo*" subtitle that adorned every cover that funny though, as it was a reference to the Palace chairman's promise to put a roof over the Holmesdale terrace to keep the elements *out* and the crowd noise *in*.

THURSDAY 11TH OCTOBER 1951

With Crystal Palace two points off the bottom of the table, the board decided to dispense with the services of joint-managers Fred Dawes and Charles Slade. Slade reverted back to his role of chief scout, but it was the end of Dawes' association with the Glaziers, a club he joined as a player in 1936 from Northampton Town.

SATURDAY 11TH OCTOBER 1980

Crystal Palace lost their seventh league game in a row, going down 1-0 away to Sunderland. It was the club's worst run since 1925.

THURSDAY 11TH OCTOBER 2007

Neil Warnock was appointed the new manager of Crystal Palace with a concise brief to avoid relegation out of the Championship.

WEDNESDAY 12TH OCTOBER 1960

Crystal Palace made the long trip up to Feethams to play Darlington in their first-ever fixture in the newly-launched Football League Cup. The Glaziers lost interest pretty quickly in the new competition, going down 2-0.

SATURDAY 12TH OCTOBER 1985

Ian Wright sealed maximum points with his first league goal for Crystal Palace as Steve Coppell's men saw off high-flying Oldham Athletic 3-2 at Selhurst. Irvine and Taylor were also on target for Palace.

WEDNESDAY 13TH OCTOBER 1954

The appointment of new Crystal Palace manager Cyril Spiers was announced to the fans via a statement in the match programme for a floodlit friendly at Selhurst Park between Crystal Palace and Scottish top-flight outfit Clyde. Spiers had played as a goalkeeper for Aston Villa, Tottenham Hotspur and Wolverhampton Wanderers and had managed at Cardiff City and Norwich City.

SATURDAY 13TH OCTOBER 1956

Johnny Byrne made his full league debut for Crystal Palace when he started at centre-forward in the Selhurst Park encounter with Swindon Town. Goalkeeper Vic Rouse, who kept a clean sheet as Palace drew 0-0, also took his bow.

SATURDAY 13TH OCTOBER 1973

Peter Taylor made his debut in the Division Two fixture away to Oxford United, a match that ended 1-1.

WEDNESDAY 14TH OCTOBER 1959

Crystal Palace made it twenty goals in two games after beating a Caribbean XI 11-1 in a friendly at Selhurst Park, four days after the 9-0 annihilation of Barrow in the league.

TUESDAY 14TH OCTOBER 1980

Terry Venables left to manage QPR after an FAlling out with Crystal Palace chairman Ray Bloye. Venables was understood to be upset about the lack of support he was getting from the board and the general lack of funds available for strengthening the squad.

SATURDAY 15TH OCTOBER 1960

Crystal Palace went to Gillingham and won 2-1, the result sent the Glaziers back to the top of the Fourth Division.

WEDNESDAY 15TH OCTOBER 1980

In the wake of Terry Venables' departure, Everton manager Howard Kendall held talks with Crystal Palace and was offered the Selhurst Park hot seat by Chairman Ray Bloye, but ultimately turned down the offer.

FRIDAY 16TH OCTOBER 1964

Crystal Palace sold goalkeeper Bill Glazier to Coventry City for £35,000, a world-record fee for a shot-stopper. Manager Dick Graham immediately replaced him with Welsh international Tony Millington, shelling out just £5,000 to West Bromwich Albion for his services.

MONDAY 16TH OCTOBER 1968

Crystal Palace ventured to Highfield Road, Coventry to face top-flight Aston Villa in a second replay of their League Cup third round tie. Without Jim Cannon, the Eagles didn't tame Andy Gray who scored a brace as the Birmingham outfit won 3-0. But the gate receipts from the 25,445 crowd allowed Terry Venables to bring Steve Kember back to Selhurst Park.

THURSDAY 16TH OCTOBER 1980

Coach Allan Harris and youth team boss George Graham jumped ship to join Terry Venables at QPR. Reserve team coach Ernie Walley was put in temporary charge, coming in at a time when Crystal Palace were in freefall in the top flight having only taken two points from a possible twenty.

SATURDAY 17TH OCTOBER 1981

Full-back Steve Lovell poked home to ensure that Palace got their first away win in 32 attempts, stretching back 19 months, when the Eagles beat Wrexham 1-0 at the Racecourse Ground.

WEDNESDAY 17TH OCTOBER 1984

Wales lost 3-0 to Spain in a World Cup qualifier in what was Peter Nicholas' last cap as a Palace player.

SATURDAY 18TH OCTOBER 1997

Crystal Palace finally ruled themselves out of an audacious bid to sign England international Paul Gascoigne from Rangers. Chairman Ron Noades spoke to representatives of both the Glasgow club and Gascoigne, and was offered a deal where Palace would take Gazza and an unnamed player for £3m. Of the deal, Noades remarked: "Frankly, we didn't want the other player but were prepared to accept that to sign Paul. Now the money is up at £4m. We'd like Paul, but not at that price." Gascoigne left Rangers for Middlesbrough on the 26th March 1998 for £3.45m.

SATURDAY 18TH OCTOBER 2003

Manager Steve Kember was left a frustrated man when Palace failed to take maximum points against ten-man Rotherham in Division One, the Eagles only able to draw 1-1 thanks to a 57th minute Dougie Freedman strike.

FRIDAY 19TH OCTOBER 2001

Steve Bruce rubbished speculation linking him with the vacant manager's job at Birmingham City. He proclaimed: "It's the last thing I need. I can't stop the speculation, I wish I could, but unfortunately it just keeps coming."

SATURDAY 19TH OCTOBER 2002

Andy Johnson scored his first goal for Palace in a 2-2 draw with Wimbledon in the Championship. Julian Gray was also on target for the Eagles as 6,358 turned out at Selhurst Park. But, the Palace fans in attendance were restless with the uninspired performance on display and sections called for manager Trevor Francis' head.

SATURDAY 20TH OCTOBER 1951

After the departure of joint-managers Fred Dawes and Charles Slade, Palace decided to go back to having a player-manger in charge. It took a five-figure sum to prise right-back Laurie Scott from Arsenal, but the former England international made an immediate impact in his first game as the lowly Glaziers beat Ipswich 3-1 in front of 21,000 at Selhurst Park.

SATURDAY 20TH OCTOBER 2001

Steve Bruce took his Palace team up to Molineux where they were looking for a seventh consecutive league win. The top-of-the-table clash was decided by Jovan Kirovski on the stroke of half-time, when his drive past Wolves keeper Michael Oakes sent the Eagles to the summit of Division One on goal difference.

SATURDAY 21ST OCTOBER 1939

Lower-league Palace faced First Division West Ham United at Upton Park on equal terms in the opening match of the new wartime league competition. Incredibly, Palace trounced the Hammers 6-2.

SATURDAY 21st OCTOBER 1989

In what ITV's Martin Tyler called a "savage piece of misjudgement" Jeff Hopkins inadvertently opened the scoring for Millwall, lobbing Perry Suckling from 25 yards. But in a thrilling South London derby, Wright and Bright grabbed a brace apiece to ensure Palace took all three points as Lions boss John Docherty chain-smoked in the dugout.

SATURDAY 22nd OCTOBER 1921

Wing-half Roy McCracken lined up alongside his brother, Newcastle defender Billy McCracken, for Northern Ireland as they faced England in the Home Championship in front of 30,000 at Windsor Park, Belfast. The game ended 1-1.

MONDAY 22nd OCTOBER 2001

Crystal Palace's league game at Coventry City was postponed to November 28th due to international call-ups.

SATURDAY 23rd OCTOBER 1920

Crystal Palace's Roy McCracken won his first cap for Ireland in a match against England at Roker Park, Sunderland, in front of 22,000 fans. Although Ireland lost 2-0, McCracken had the distinction of becoming the first international from the newly-formed Third Division.

MONDAY 23rd OCTOBER 2000

Dougie Freedman returned to Palace, as Alan Smith paid Nottingham Forest £600,000 in order for the prodigal son to return home.

TUESDAY 24th OCTOBER 1978

Second Division Leicester City received £40,000 as Steve Kember returned to Selhurst Park.

SATURDAY 24th OCTOBER 1998

Palace's Division One fixture against Bradford City at Valley Parade was called off at half-time by Scarborough referee Bill Burn due to adverse weather conditions – the pitch resembled a lake. Palace had taken the lead after eight minutes when Clinton Morrison poked home from close range only for the Bantams to equalise in the 28th minute when Isaiah Rankin turned home Robbie Blake's low cross.

CLINTON MORRISON CELEBRATES HIS 'GOAL' AT BRADFORD

FRIDAY 25TH OCTOBER 1996

Neil Shipperley joined Crystal Palace for the first time, moving to Selhurst Park at a cost of £1.2m from Premiership Southampton.

WEDNESDAY 25TH OCTOBER 2000

After watching his team lose to Grimsby Town 1-0 the previous night, in front of 16,685 at Selhurst Park, furious manager Alan Smith transfer-listed Clinton Morrison, Hayden Mullins and Jamie Smith.

WEDNESDAY 26TH OCTOBER 2005

Speaking the morning after the Eagles beat Liverpool, current Champions of Europe, in the third round of the League Cup, Man of the Match, goalkeeper Julian Speroni said: "Now we must forget about this result and get back to training hard and doing what we've be doing so far." The result and subsequent reports were relayed around the world on *BBC World Service* and heard by the author's brother in Sri Lanka!

SATURDAY 26TH OCTOBER 2002

Crystal Palace faced their bitter south coast rivals Brighton & Hove Albion for the first time in over 13 years in the league, in what was a must-win game for under-fire Palace gaffer Trevor Francis. With 21,796 inside Selhurst Park, the atmosphere was electric. Thankfully, the Palace players knew what this game meant to the fans and promptly tore Brighton apart. Andy Johnson opened the scoring after just four minutes and went on to nail a hat-trick in under an hour to become an instant Palace legend. Dougie Freedman and Julian Gray also got on the scoresheet as Palace were rampant against a side managed by former favourite Steve Coppell. The 5-0 scoreline was quite simply Trevor Francis' finest hour as manager.

TUESDAY 27TH OCTOBER 1953

French Ligue One side Stade Francais provided the first international opposition to play under Selhurst Park's new floodlights. Crystal Palace won 4-2.

SATURDAY 27TH OCTOBER 1990

Crystal Palace beat Wimbledon 4-3 at Selhurst Park and set a new record for the best start by a new top-flight club, that of ten games undefeated.

WEDNESDAY 27TH OCTOBER 1999

Crystal Palace legend Johnny Byrne passed away in Cape Town.

WEDNESDAY 27TH OCTOBER 2004

Sandor Torghelle scored his only goal in Crystal Palace colours as Iain Dowie's men dumped Charlton Athletic out of the League Cup at the third round stage, the Eagles winning 2-1. Torghelle was sent off after he received his second caution for a blatant dive.

SATURDAY 28TH OCTOBER 1978

Referee Edward Hughes blew his whistle for full-time five and a half minutes too early after his watch stopped in the league encounter between Crystal Palace and Fulham at Selhurst Park. With half the 28,733 crowd on their way home thinking the Eagles had lost 1-0 and the teams themselves in the dressing rooms with their boots off, Hughes' linesman pointed out the error. Hughes then made both teams return to the pitch to finish the game, but Venables' men couldn't take advantage and still lost after 90 minutes.

SATURDAY 28TH OCTOBER 2000

Dougie Freedman scored a brace in his second game back at Crystal Palace following his £600,000 move from Nottingham Forest, as the Eagles shared in six goals away at promotion hopefuls Bolton Wanderers. But, it was Clinton Morrison who scored the all-important equaliser in the 90th minute which earned Palace a point in the Division One clash at the Reebok Stadium.

TUESDAY 29TH OCTOBER 1974

Just three minutes into his England under-23 debut, Peter Taylor opened the scoring against Czechoslovakia. His ninth minute free-kick was then converted by Mick Mills as Don Revie's men strolled to a 3-1 victory in a European under-23 Championship qualifier played at Selhurst Park.

TUESDAY 29TH OCTOBER 2002

Andy Johnson scored his second ever hat-trick for Palace as they came from behind to beat Colin Lee's Walsall 4-3 in a Division One encounter at the Bescot Stadium. AJ's first three-goal haul had come four days earlier in the 5-0 annihilation of Brighton & Hove Albion.

WEDNESDAY 30TH OCTOBER 1974

Palace defender Paddy Mulligan turned out for the Republic of Ireland in their 3-0 victory over the Soviet Union in a European Championship qualifier in Dublin.

THURSDAY 30TH OCTOBER 1997

Ivano Bonetti left Crystal Palace having only played 50 minutes of first team football for the Eagles. The former Sampdoria and Grimsby Town midfielder signed a deal with Italian Serie B club Genoa.

MONDAY 31ST OCTOBER 1921

In a London Challenge Cup tie against Charlton Athletic at The Nest there was a fire in the grandstand during the game. But it didn't stop the match from being completed and Crystal Palace won 2-1.

SATURDAY 31ST OCTOBER 1981

Crystal Palace signed striker Kevin Mabbutt from Bristol City for £200,000, but the Eagles would lose on his debut – 1-0 at Luton Town.

WEDNESDAY 31ST OCTOBER 2001

High-flying Crystal Palace were stunned by West Bromwich Albion in the league at Selhurst Park when veteran striker Bob Taylor stole the points for the Baggies in the 63rd minute. But the home crowd were given something to cheer about when Wayne Routledge was given his first senior appearance, coming on as an 88th minute substitute for Jovan Kirovski. At the time, Routledge went into the record books as the third-youngest player ever to appear for Palace, behind only Phil Hoadley and Kenny Sansom.

CRYSTAL PALACE
On This Day

NOVEMBER

SATURDAY 1st NOVEMBER 1962

Cam Burgess and Johnny Rainford both hit hat-tricks as Crystal Palace twice came from behind to beat Swindon Town 6-3 in a league encounter at the County Ground.

SATURDAY 1st NOVEMBER 1980

After an angry deputation of players led by Jim Cannon demanded that the board give temporary gaffer Ernie Walley the permanent job, Ray Bloye responded by appointing Walley as caretaker manager for the rest of the season.

THURSDAY 1st NOVEMBER 2001

Steve Bruce resigned as Crystal Palace manager in order to take over at Division One rivals Birmingham City but chairman Simon Jordan refused to accept his resignation.

SATURDAY 2nd NOVEMBER 1935

Crystal Palace thumped local rivals Millwall 5-0 in front of 19,239 in the league at Selhurst Park, with manager Tom Bromilow seeing debutants Bob Birtley and Jack Blackman both find the net. Striker Albert Dawes also weighed in with a hat-trick.

SATURDAY 2nd NOVEMBER 1991

Two seasons after a 9-0 drubbing at Anfield in the league, Steve Coppell sent out a Crystal Palace side that took three points off Liverpool in front of their own supporters. Glenn Hysen may have headed the Reds in front, but new boy Marco Gabbiadini soon restored parity allowing Geoff Thomas to head the winner following Eric Young's flick-on from a corner.

WEDNESDAY 3rd NOVEMBER 1920

Crystal Palace lost 3-2 to a physical Southend United side at The Nest, but the game was marred by a pitch invasion as the home fans vented their anger and surrounded the opposition players and officials. Called to account by the FA for alleged assaults on Southend player Fairclough and the referee, Palace offered the defence that the visiting right-back had played a "constantly over-vigorous match". Punishment was duly dished out with The Nest being closed for a fortnight and Palace banned from playing within a ten-mile radius of their home ground.

MONDAY 3RD NOVEMBER 2003

Steve Kember was sacked as Palace manager after a string of poor performances that culminated in a 5-0 thrashing at the hands of Wigan in a televised fixture. Player-coach Kit Symons stepped up to the role of caretaker player-manager.

SATURDAY 4TH NOVEMBER 1978

South Norwood-born Nick Chatterton scored in the 2-1 defeat away at Burnley, in what was Steve Kember's first game back at Palace since he rejoined from Leicester City.

SATURDAY 4TH NOVEMBER 1972

Don Rogers scored the only goal of the game on his debut when Palace beat Everton 1-0 to gain their third win of the season and move off the bottom of the table. Glaziers manager Bert Head knew Rogers from when he managed at Swindon Town, and persuaded the Wiltshire outfit to part with their star man in return for £150,000.

TUESDAY 4TH NOVEMBER 1980

Stepney-born Republic of Ireland international Jerry Murphy asked manager Ernie Walley for a transfer.

SUNDAY 4TH NOVEMBER 2001

Simon Jordan agreed that manager Steve Bruce could leave for Birmingham City, but only on terms favourable to the Palace chairman.

SATURDAY 5TH NOVEMBER 1960

Former Palace manager Laurie Scott returned to Selhurst Park when he took his Hitchin Town side to South London for an FA Cup first round match. There was no room for sentiment as Palace saw off the amateurs 6-2.

FRIDAY 5TH NOVEMBER 2004

Palace manager Iain Dowie, along with Andy Johnson, Shaun Derry and Danny Butterfield, officially opened the new Thornton Heath Leisure Centre.

SATURDAY 5TH NOVEMBER 2005

Gabor Kiraly remonstrated with the referee when he felt former Eagle Neil Shipperley's controversial headed winner for Sheffield United did not cross the line. But the goal stood and the Blades nicked a 3-2 win at Selhurst Park in the Championship. Phil Jagielka and Paul Ifill were the other scorers for Neil Warnock's men, whilst Michael Hughes and Dougie Freedman were on target for Palace.

SATURDAY 6TH NOVEMBER 1909

George Whitworth put four past New Brompton in a Southern League, Division One fixture.

TUESDAY 6TH NOVEMBER 2001

Aki Riihilahti was a bit too optimistic when he went on record about the Eagles' promotion chances: "I always thought we were good enough to be there, in the play-off places, and I think we can be there at the end of the season."

TUESDAY 6TH NOVEMBER 2007

Victor Moses made his first-team debut away at Cardiff City in the Championship, replacing fellow youngster John Bostock after 72 minutes. Moses' strength and pace caused the Bluebirds a few issues late on, but the England under-18s introduction wasn't enough to snatch a win, Neil Warnock forced to settle for a point when Ben Watson's 44th minute penalty levelled matters at Ninian Park.

WEDNESDAY 7TH NOVEMBER 2001

The FA announced that two high profile women's matches – the FA Cup Final and World Cup qualifier between England and Germany – would be held at Selhurst Park. FA Head of Women's Football Karen Doyle said: "We deliberately chose Selhurst because last year's cup there was a storming success."

WEDNESDAY 7TH NOVEMBER 2001

Steve Kember and Terry Bullivant signed four-year contracts as they took charge of team affairs following Steve Bruce's attempted resignation. It had been reported that Bruce was trying to tempt the two of them to move to the Midlands club with him.

MONDAY 8TH NOVEMBER 1976

Former Aston Villa, Chelsea, Arsenal and Manchester United midfielder George Graham arrived at Palace from Portsmouth in a deal that saw striker David Kemp head to the south coast.

WEDNESDAY 8TH NOVEMBER 1989

Assistant manager Stan Ternent quit Crystal Palace to become manager of Second Division Hull City. Reserve and youth team boss Alan Smith, who had been with the club since 1983 and helped to develop the likes of Richard Shaw and John Salako, was promoted in his place.

MONDAY 9TH NOVEMBER 1970

An under-strength Palace visited Arsenal for a fourth round replay in the Football League Cup. A Highbury crowd of 45,026 were stunned when Gerry Queen and Bobby Tambling helped Palace to an FAmous 2-0 win, for the Gunners only suffered this one defeat at home all season when they stormed to the double.

SATURDAY 9TH NOVEMBER 2002

In a clash of Division One's form sides, Crystal Palace and Nottingham Forest played out a 0-0 draw at Selhurst Park. The result meant the Eagles went unbeaten in nine games, whilst Forest made it ten straight without loss in the league. Andy Johnson went into the game with ten goals in his last five starts, but never looked likely to add to his tally against a Forest defence superbly marshalled by the evergreen Des Walker.

MONDAY 10TH NOVEMBER 1980

Vince Hilaire and Gerry Francis handed in transfer requests. Ernie Walley rejected them both.

TUESDAY 10TH NOVEMBER 1981

Dario Gradi was sacked as Palace languished in 15th place in the Second Division. Gradi was in charge for a total of 27 games, winning just six. Youth team coach Steve Kember was immediately promoted to the hot seat.

SATURDAY 11TH NOVEMBER 1961

Andy Smillie scored a hat-trick as Palace hammered Grimsby Town 4-1 in a Division Three fixture at Selhurst Park.

SATURDAY 11TH NOVEMBER 1978

Midfielder Nick Chatterton was left out of the side that eased past Blackburn Rovers 3-0 at Selhurst Park. The son of former groundsman Len Chatterton requested a transfer and was moved quickly to near neighbours Millwall where he became their club captain. Chatterton made 183 appearances for Palace and scored 36 times.

SATURDAY 11TH NOVEMBER 2000

Clinton Morrison, placed on the transfer list by Alan Smith, scored twice after Dougie Freedman had opened the scoring as Palace continued their climb away from the bottom of Division One with a 3-1 win over Wolves at Molineux.

THURSDAY 12TH NOVEMBER 1953

David Harris resigned as chairman of Crystal Palace and was succeeded by Arthur Wait, who was elected to the position for the first time.

WEDNESDAY 12TH NOVEMBER 1986

Steve Coppell and Ron Noades drove up to Maine Road to watch Manchester City reserves take on Leicester City in order to watch Mark Bright, on the recommendation of scout John Griffin. Bright scored a hat-trick for the Foxes; Coppell and Noades pledged to buy him.

MONDAY 12TH NOVEMBER 2001

Matters took a turn for the worse in the Steve Bruce saga when chairman Simon Jordan issued a court injunction against the suspended manager in an attempt to stop him joining Birmingham City.

MONDAY 13TH NOVEMBER 1905

Peter Simpson was born in Leith, Scotland. He joined Crystal Palace from Kettering in June 1929 and was one of the best forwards to ever play for the club. Simpson scored an incredible 165 goals in 195 appearances. He later played for West Ham United and Reading before retiring to take over a newsagent and tobacconists in West Croydon.

THURSDAY 13TH NOVEMBER 1986

Steve Coppell and Ron Noades agreed personal terms with Mark Bright in a service station on the M1. Coppell told the Stoke-born forward that he knew his partnership with his new strike partner Ian would work out, simply because their names sounded so brilliant together…

SATURDAY 14TH NOVEMBER 1959

Johnny Byrne scored his second-ever hat-trick for Crystal Palace when the Glaziers beat non-league Chelmsford City 5-1 at Selhurst Park in the first round of the FA Cup. The next round saw Palace at Margate.

SATURDAY 14TH NOVEMBER 1970

Having beaten Arsenal at Highbury five days earlier in the League Cup, Crystal Palace returned for their league encounter and earned a 1-1 draw against the side who marched to the title.

SATURDAY 15TH NOVEMBER 1924

George Whitworth scored the last of three hat-tricks for Crystal Palace when he found the net three times in a 4-1 win over Bradford City in a Division Two fixture at Selhurst Park.

SATURDAY 15TH NOVEMBER 1986

Mark Bright scored the Palace opener on his debut when the Eagles drew 3-3 at home to Ipswich Town. Ian Wright also scored. The most famous strike partnership in Crystal Palace history was born.

SATURDAY 16TH NOVEMBER 1963

Eastern Counties outfit Harwich & Parkestone were smashed 8-2 in the first round of the FA Cup at Selhurst Park. The result against the Essex side, formed in 1877, remains Palace's highest-ever score in the famous old cup competition.

MONDAY 16TH NOVEMBER 1953

Colonel Trevor, one of the original seven men who took control of Crystal Palace in January 1950, resigned from his position as director.

WEDNESDAY 16TH NOVEMBER 2005

Tony Popovic helped Australia to the 2006 World Cup in Germany when their qualifying play-off match against Uruguay went to penalties.

SATURDAY 17TH NOVEMBER 1956

Crystal Palace's first cup-tie under floodlights was staged when they took on Isthmian League outfit Walthamstow Avenue in the first round of the FA Cup. Palace won the tie against the amateurs, who were early forerunners of Dagenham & Redbridge, 2-0.

FRIDAY 17TH NOVEMBER 1995

Player of The Year Richard Shaw joined ex-Eagle John Salako at Premiership Coventry City. Palace were remunerated to the tune of £1m.

WEDNESDAY 18TH NOVEMBER 1981

Steve Coppell picked up the knee injury that forced his early retirement from the game when playing for England against Hungary in a World Cup qualifier in front of 92,000 at Wembley.

TUESDAY 18TH NOVEMBER 1997

Michele Padovano signed for Crystal Palace from Juventus for £1.7m. The Italian forward had scored in the penalty shoot-out in the Champions League final just over a year earlier when Juventus beat Ajax.

MONDAY 19TH NOVEMBER 2001

Another 'Fans Night' was scheduled with Hayden Mullins, Aki Riihilahti and Gary O'Reilly in attendance. Elsewhere Christian Edwards, on loan from Nottingham Forest, stated that contrary to media reports, "Steve Kember and Terry Bullivant have been fantastic and training is enjoyable".

WEDNESDAY 19TH NOVEMBER 1975

Ian Evans won the first of 13 caps for Wales when he played for his country in their 1-0 European Championship qualifier win over Austria at Wrexham.

SATURDAY 20TH NOVEMBER 1976

A late Rachid Harkouk equaliser in front of 30,000 fans at the Goldstone Ground in the first round of the FA Cup ensured Palace were able to take the Seagulls back to Selhurst Park for a replay.

SUNDAY 20TH NOVEMBER 2005

Dougie Freedman scored his 100th and 101st goals as Crystal Palace beat Brighton & Hove Albion at Withdean Stadium 3-2 in the Championship, but it was Jobi McAnuff who sealed the points with a sweet 90th minute winner.

SATURDAY 21ST NOVEMBER 1953

For the second season in a row, Palace were knocked out of the FA Cup by a non-league side. This time it was Great Yarmouth who dispatched the Glaziers 1-0 in the first round at Wellesley Recreation Ground.

TUESDAY 21ST NOVEMBER 1989

Nigel Martyn became the country's first £1m goalkeeper when he signed from Bristol Rovers.

WEDNESDAY 22ND NOVEMBER 1961

Johnny Byrne lined up alongside Bobby Charlton and Johnny Haynes to win his first England cap whilst with Third Division Crystal Palace. The occasion was a Home International Championship fixture against Northern Ireland at Wembley, and the 30,000 crowd witnessed a 1-1 draw. Byrne was Palace's first full England international since John Alderson in May 1923.

THURSDAY 22ND NOVEMBER 2001

A Crystal Palace reserve team faced Latvian side Skonto Riga in a friendly at Beckenham at 1pm. Fellow countrymen and Eagles players Andrejs Rubins and Aleksandrs Kolinko both turned out for Palace.

SATURDAY 22ND NOVEMBER 1975

Crystal Palace squeaked past Isthmian League side Walton & Hersham in the first round of the FA Cup thanks to a solitary close range strike from David Kemp, who went up against a number of his former Slough teammates in the opposing side.

TUESDAY 23RD NOVEMBER 1976

Palace drew 1-1 with Alan Mullery's Brighton & Hove Albion at Selhurst Park in an FA Cup first round replay to set up a third meeting between the two rivals at Stamford Bridge.

THURSDAY 23rd NOVEMBER 2000

Palace's hopes of signing Steve Staunton for a further loan period hit a snag when the Irishman played for Liverpool in their Uefa Cup tie with Greek outfit Olympiakos.

FRIDAY 23rd NOVEMBER 2001

Simon Jordan announced Ian Wright would return to the club, working once a week with the strikers at Beckenham. Jordan said: "Ian is an interesting and exciting character, who will add plenty of fizz to training, but there has been no mention of him becoming a manager – it is not a job he wants to do."

SATURDAY 24th NOVEMBER 1951

The wheels started to come off Laurie Scott's Palace tenure less than two months after moving to Selhurst Park when the Glaziers were knocked out of the FA Cup by Gillingham.

SATURDAY 24th NOVEMBER 1928

Palace comfortably saw off non-league Kettering Town 2-0 in the first round of the FA Cup, but the remarkable fact about the fixture was that Palace later signed a number of the Kettering team who had impressed that day. Goalkeeper Jim Imrie, inside-forward Andy Dunsire and winger/centre-forward George Charlesworth joined in March 1929 but it was the capture of Peter Simpson in June that proved the most significant. Simpson scored 165 goals in 195 appearances until his transfer to West Ham in 1935, and became Palace's all-time leading goalscorer in the process.

TUESDAY 24th NOVEMBER 1981

Steve Kember's first home match in charge as manager saw Kevin Mabbutt bag a brace in a 2-1 win over Norwich City. But the crowds had well and truly drifted away from Selhurst Park as not even Kember's presence at the helm could inspire a five-figure crowd, as just 9,010 turned up.

SATURDAY 25th NOVEMBER 1950

A first round FA Cup tie against Millwall was abandoned after half an hour with the score at 0-0 when fog enveloped Selhurst Park. For the majority of the 24,000 present it was a blessing in disguise as the Lions were the better team.

WEDNESDAY 25TH NOVEMBER 1987

After being unsettled by Aston Villa, Andy Gray moved to the Midlands club for £150,000, just as Palace looked to shape up for a sustained assault on promotion.

WEDNESDAY 26TH NOVEMBER 1969

Sir Alf Ramsey officially opened the new Arthur Wait stand ahead of former manager Arthur Rowe's testimonial. The actual match saw Palace lose 5-3 to an International XI.

WEDNESDAY 26TH NOVEMBER 1962

Arthur Rowe was sidelined through illness, so assistant Dick Graham took over the reins to become the new Crystal Palace manager. His first match in charge wasn't pleasant as the Glaziers crashed out of the FA Cup 7-2 away to Mansfield Town following a second round replay.

SATURDAY 26TH NOVEMBER 1983

A rare high point in a mediocre campaign occurred when Palace beat Sheffield Wednesday, previously unbeaten all season. David Giles was the man who did the damage as the Eagles won 1-0 at Selhurst.

SATURDAY 27TH NOVEMBER 1920

With The Nest closed due to crowd trouble, Palace had to play their home fixture against Exeter City at The Dell, Southampton, and won 2-1. Palace could have played at either White Hart Lane, Tottenham or Clapton Orient's ground at Millfields Road, East London but weren't quick enough in taking up either option.

TUESDAY 27TH NOVEMBER 2007

Clinton Morrison and Clint Hill were both on target when Crystal Palace beat Preston North End 2-1 at Selhurst Park in the Championship. It was only Neil Warnock's second win since taking charge of the Eagles in October.

SATURDAY 28TH NOVEMBER 1925

In a Division Three (South) fixture on a snow-covered pitch, Crystal Palace drew 5-5 with Plymouth Argyle in the highest-scoring draw a first-class game at Selhurst Park had ever produced.

SATURDAY 28TH NOVEMBER 1992

Crystal Palace found themselves next-to-bottom in the Premier League after getting thrashed 5-0 by Liverpool at Anfield in front of 36,380.

WEDNESDAY 29TH NOVEMBER 1950

Crystal Palace lost 4-1 at home to Millwall in the first round of the FA Cup, and coupled with the Glaziers' position at the foot of the league, it was enough to cost Ronnie Rooke his job as Palace manager that evening. Rooke's big spending had failed to produce results on the pitch, and the associated large wage bill he had run up proved too much for chairman David Harris and the new board.

SATURDAY 29TH NOVEMBER 1980

Crystal Palace lost 3-2 at home to Manchester City. Former Eagles manager Malcolm Allison was watching ominously from the stand, having been linked with the role again.

SATURDAY 29TH NOVEMBER 1986

In the author of this book's first game, Mark Bright grabbed his second Crystal Palace goal to seal a 2-0 win against Sunderland after Tony Finnigan had put the Eagles ahead. The match also saw a dog run on the pitch from the sparsely populated Whitehorse Lane terrace.

SUNDAY 30TH NOVEMBER 1952

New manager Dick Graham responded to allegations that he had a dirty team by stating: "Palace had tried to play so much football early in the season that the sudden determination I introduced into the side probably came as a surprise to clubs who thought they were on an easy touch."

FRIDAY 30TH NOVEMBER 2001

Crystal Palace appointed Trevor Francis as their new manager, who had been out of work since leaving Birmingham City in mid-October to make way for Steve Bruce. Bruce was still suspended from the manager's role at Selhurst Park after he had tried to resign in order to move to the Blues. Officially, Bruce was also still on gardening leave, having to serve out his notice before he moved up to the West Midlands club.

CRYSTAL PALACE
On This Day

DECEMBER

TUESDAY 1st DECEMBER 1936

After little more than five months in charge of first team affairs, former director R S Moyes resigned as Crystal Palace manager after growing frustrated with the dealings of a couple of incoming transfers. A week later the chairman Carey Burnett also resigned as chaos reigned at Selhurst Park. Star striker Albert Dawes was also allowed to leave for Luton Town in the confusion.

MONDAY 1st DECEMBER 1980

Malcolm Allison met with the Crystal Palace board and agreed to return to Selhurst Park as joint manager with Ernie Walley.

SATURDAY 1st DECEMBER 2001

New manager Trevor Francis had a poor start to his Crystal Palace career when his new team lost 2-1 to Burnley at home in the league.

SATURDAY 2nd DECEMBER 1950

In the wake of Ronnie Rooke's sacking, the Crystal Palace board opted to appoint joint-managers, promoting assistant manager Fred Dawes and scout Charlie Slade to the helm of the club. The duo reluctantly accepted what proved to be a thankless task, but they started their mission impossible brightly enough with a 1-0 home win over Walsall, Palace's first win in eight games. The scorer of the goal was Trevor Herbert, a 21-year-old centre-forward who was only given his debut at the behest of the club directors.

TUESDAY 2nd DECEMBER 1980

Malcolm Allison became sole Crystal Palace manager with Ernie Walley as his assistant, just a day after the two men were paraded as joint managers.

MONDAY 3rd DECEMBER 2001

A reserve game with QPR at Dulwich was called off due to a waterlogged pitch but the 'Fans Night' went ahead at Selhurst Park with Julian Gray, Dean Austin and academy director Derek Broadley in attendance.

SATURDAY 3rd DECEMBER 2005

Palace drew 1-1 against Millwall at Selhurst Park in the Championship when Lions fan Ben Watson saved face with a 90th minute equaliser.

TUESDAY 4TH DECEMBER 2001

Coach Terry Bullivant stated: "Trevor Francis has come in and we all seem to be getting on very well – we told him that he won't work for a better group of supporters."

SUNDAY 4TH DECEMBER 2005

Palace were drawn at home to either Stevenage Borough or Northampton Town in the third round of the FA Cup.

SATURDAY 5TH DECEMBER 1959

Palace travelled to Hartsdown Park to face Margate in a tricky FA Cup second round tie. On a pudding of a pitch, the Glaziers escaped with a 0-0 draw but it was the watching scouts who drew the most looks as interest began to mount in Johnny Byrne who had put in a transfer request, albeit one that was turned down by the board.

TUESDAY 5TH DECEMBER 1989

Steve Coppell paid Division Two outfit Newcastle United £650,000 for their former Wimbledon centre-back, Carshalton-born Andy Thorn.

SATURDAY 6TH DECEMBER 1952

Thick fog saved Palace from a humiliating away defeat at the hands of Finchley, who were 3-1 ahead in an FA Cup second round tie, when the referee abandoned the game in the 61st minute. The Glaziers were without Bob Thomas and Les Devonshire who had got lost on their way to North London and had phoned ahead to admit they were stranded at Park Royal. Laurie Scott subsequently had a message broadcast around Finchley's ground for any Palace players who were in the crowd to report to the dressing room as they were needed, but of those who turned up only Bob Bishop was used due to his feet being able to fit in Devonshire's boots!

SATURDAY 6TH DECEMBER 1997

Palace were denied a sixth away win in the Premiership when Leicester City's Muzzy Izzet grabbed a last-gasp equaliser at Filbert Street following Michele Padovano's first goal for the Eagles. Palace had played with ten men following Marc Edworthy's sending-off with just 29 minutes gone.

MONDAY 6TH DECEMBER 1976

Stamford Bridge was the setting as Palace finally overcame Brighton & Hove Albion at the third time of asking in the FA Cup first round. The south coast side had a goal disallowed and were forced to retake a penalty that was then saved, which prompted manager Alan Mullery to berate referee Ron Challis for his decisions, then offer Palace fans two fingers before ending his performance by throwing down a fiver's worth of notes into a puddle and screaming: "You're not worth that, Palace," before being led away by the police down the tunnel. Mullery was fined £75 for his actions as the modern-day rivalry between the two clubs really heated up.

FRIDAY 7TH DECEMBER 2001

Palace completed the permanent signing of Kit Symons from Fulham after agreeing personal terms. Sean Hankin joined Torquay.

SATURDAY 7TH DECEMBER 2002

Danny Granville was the hero when his 73rd minute, 20-yard free-kick was the only goal of the game in the derby fixture with Millwall at Selhurst Park. The match itself was a niggly encounter with six yellow cards shown by referee Phil Dowd.

MONDAY 8TH DECEMBER 1924

Future Palace manager Jack Butler won his only England cap in a 4-0 friendly win against Belgium in front of 15,405 at The Hawthorns, West Bromwich.

SATURDAY 8TH DECEMBER 1906

Palace entered the FA Cup at the fifth qualifying round stage, but their fixture against Rotherham County had to be switched to Stamford Bridge due to the Crystal Palace hosting a rugby union fixture between England and South Africa. Palace duly did the business over in West London, dispatching the Yorkshire club 4-0 to put themselves into the draw for the first round proper.

SATURDAY 8TH DECEMBER 1979

Palace the best team in Europe? Maybe not, but they did beat the reigning European Cup holders Nottingham Forest in a league encounter at Selhurst Park, Brian Clough's men going down 1-0.

SATURDAY 9TH DECEMBER 1989

Palace took four points off Manchester United for the season when they beat Alex Ferguson's men 2-1 at Old Trafford thanks to a brace from Mark Bright. The game also marked Andy Thorn's debut for the club.

SATURDAY 9TH DECEMBER 2000

Clinton Morrison snaffled up his 13th goal of the season as Crystal Palace beat Watford 1-0 at Selhurst Park in the league, condemning the Hertfordshire club to their fifth successive defeat. The Eagles were on a good run of form, having not lost since October.

MONDAY 10TH DECEMBER 1962

Two weeks into the job, and with Palace at the foot of the table, new Crystal Palace manager Dick Graham faced a mini rebellion when a petition signed by 13 senior players, protesting against his methods, was handed to the board of directors. The complaint was immediately rejected by the Selhurst Park bosses and they backed the former Palace goalkeeper to turn things around.

WEDNESDAY 10TH DECEMBER 1952

Palace lost 3-1 away to amateur outfit Finchley of the Athenian League in the FA Cup second round after the original fixture was abandoned due to fog.

SATURDAY 11TH DECEMBER 1954

Northern League amateurs Bishop Auckland knocked Palace out of the FA Cup in the second round, winning 4-2 in front of 20,000 at Selhurst Park. Auckland also missed a penalty!

SATURDAY 11TH DECEMBER 1920

The Nest was reopened following crowd trouble against Southend United but Palace failed to rise to the occasion and lost 1-0 to Swansea, with home favourite and Irish international Roy McCracken breaking his leg.

SATURDAY 11TH DECEMBER 1976

After coming through *that* epic and infamous first round tie with Brighton & Hove Albion, Crystal Palace faced amateur outfit Enfield at Selhurst Park, and promptly beat them 4-0.

THURSDAY 11TH DECEMBER 1980

Crystal Palace accounts revealed they made more than £1m from the Sainsbury's store deal at Selhurst Park.

SATURDAY 12TH DECEMBER 1964

Keith Smith, signed from Peterborough United the month before, took just six seconds to score against Derby County at the Baseball Ground in a match that Crystal Palace eventually drew 3-3. It was one of the fastest goals ever recorded in world football.

WEDNESDAY 12TH DECEMBER 1956

Crystal Palace's biggest crowd since the war, 23,137, turned up to see the Glaziers beat Brentford 3-2 in an FA Cup second round replay to set up a tie away to Millwall.

FRIDAY 12TH DECEMBER 1947

Ahead of Crystal Palace's FA Cup second round tie against Bristol City at Ashton Gate, manager Jack Butler took his team to Brighton for sea water baths, massage, a walk along the front, lunch and an afternoon matinee show.

SATURDAY 12TH DECEMBER 1931

Crystal Palace exited the FA Cup at the hands of a non-league club for the first time, courtesy of Bath City on a sticky Twerton Park pitch. Palace had been coasting in the second round tie, taking the lead through Peter Simpson after just 15 minutes. But a retaken penalty had seen Bath back on terms, and they secured themselves an FAmous victory with a close-range winner five minutes from time.

TUESDAY 12TH DECEMBER 1989

Ian Wright made his England 'B' debut against Yugoslavia 'B' at The Den, the ground of the club he grew up supporting as a boy, Millwall. But Wright did not do his talents justice and was pulled off at half-time, having been racially abused by elements of the 8,231 crowd. Wright made four appearances for the senior team as a Palace player.

SATURDAY 13TH DECEMBER 1958

Inside-forward Roy Summersby, signed from Millwall, netted on his debut for Crystal Palace in their 2-0 league win against Walsall. Johnny Byrne scored the other that day at Selhurst Park, and it was to be the first of many great performances from the Palace front-line partnership.

SATURDAY 13TH DECEMBER 1947

Palace beat Bristol City 1-0 at Ashton Gate in the FA Cup second round. The only goal of the game was scored in the 111th minute by Bert Robson. The FA allowed extra time if required in an effort to avoid midweek replays in the austerity of a post-war Britain.

SATURDAY 13TH DECEMBER 1975

Palace faced a replay in the second round of the FA Cup after drawing 1-1 with Millwall at The Den.

WEDNESDAY 14TH DECEMBER 1994

Palace's Chris Coleman featured for Wales when they were beaten 3-0 by Bulgaria in a European Championship qualifier in Cardiff.

FRIDAY 14TH DECEMBER 2001

The Selhurst Park Club Shop stayed open until 9pm as Andrejs Rubins and Andrew Martin signed autographs.

MONDAY 15TH DECEMBER 1980

Terry Fenwick and Mike Flanagan left for QPR in a deal worth £250,000. Defender Fenwick made 82 appearances for Palace and scored two goals, whilst centre-forward Flanagan managed 13 strikes from his 64 games.

SATURDAY 15TH DECEMBER 1984

Andy Gray, signed from Dulwich Hamlet for £2,000 the month before, scored on his full debut in a 3-1 win away at Grimsby Town.

FRIDAY 15TH DECEMBER 1995

Chris Coleman departed Selhurst Park to join up with the Premiership champions Blackburn Rovers in a £2.75m transfer. The Welshman had joined Palace as a defender but had been used up front when circumstances dictated, scoring 16 goals in 190 appearances.

SATURDAY 16TH DECEMBER 1972

Palace thrashed Manchester United 5-0 in a Division One fixture at Selhurst Park, right-back Paddy Mulligan started the rout with a ninth-minute opener before he claimed his brace three minutes before half-time. Don Rogers scored his second goal in two games just a minute after the restart, before Alan Whittle made it 4-0 when he scored on his debut. Rogers then rounded Alex Stepney and made it five without reply. Three days later the Old Trafford board sacked manager Frank O'Farrell.

TUESDAY 16TH DECEMBER 1975

Palace reached the third round of the FA Cup after beating Millwall 2-1 in a replay at Selhurst Park.

SATURDAY 16TH DECEMBER 1989

Palace played their first ever 'away' game at Selhurst Park in the first of the always entitled 'Landlord versus Tenant' fixtures. Coppell's men won 2-1 after Andy Thorn set the Eagles on their way with his first goal for the club. Mark Bright scored the second. 'Away' fans were housed in the Arthur Wait stand.

WEDNESDAY 16TH DECEMBER 1992

Palace may have been struggling in the Premier League, but their form in the League Cup was decent enough. Liverpool came to Selhurst for a replay after Coppell's men had held them 1-1 at Anfield, and in front of 16,622 Palace dismissed Graeme Souness' side 2-1 thanks to goals from youngster Grant Watts and Andy Thorn.

SATURDAY 16TH DECEMBER 1995

Gareth Taylor scored his only league goal for Palace, the winning strike in a 2-1 victory away to Stoke in the First Division.

WEDNESDAY 17TH DECEMBER 1930

Peter Simpson scored four as Crystal Palace smashed Watford 6-1 at Selhurst Park in a Division Three (South) fixture. Four days earlier Palace had scored six without reply against Newark Town in the FA Cup.

SATURDAY 17TH DECEMBER 1938

Albert Ronson scored his one and only hat-trick for Crystal Palace as the Glaziers dismissed Mansfield Town 6-2 in a Division Three (South) clash at Selhurst Park.

WEDNESDAY 17TH DECEMBER 1980

Fulham chairman, Yorkshireman Ernie Clay, made a bid for Ray Bloye's shares, but the Palace chairman rebuffed him and insisted: "I'm staying." Clay later acquired the freehold to Craven Cottage before selling up in 1987 to David Bulstrode of Marler Estates, who already owned the Stamford Bridge stadium and QPR football club. Bulstrode's aim was to merge Fulham with QPR and create a new team called Fulham Park Rangers playing out of Loftus Road.

WEDNESDAY 18TH DECEMBER 1935

Crystal Palace beat the original Newport County 6-0 in a Division Three (South) game at Selhurst Park. Jack Blackman scored his first hat-trick for the club.

FRIDAY 18TH DECEMBER 1998

In a newspaper interview, Mark Goldberg dismissed reports that he was in any sort of financial trouble whilst waving away rumours that Wimbledon might buy Selhurst Park. He also confirmed that *Tramp Oil and Marine* were poised to facilitate a £2m investment in the club.

SATURDAY 18TH DECEMBER 2004

Gabor Kiraly saved a penalty from Wayne Rooney at Old Trafford in a Premiership fixture against Manchester United whilst Danny Granville and Joonas Kolkka both got themselves on the scoresheet, but despite all that, Palace still managed to lose 5-2 in front of 67,814 fans to find themselves back in the bottom three of the top flight.

FRIDAY 19TH DECEMBER 1990

Another Palace player switched to QPR to rejoin Terry Venables. This time it was goalkeeper John Burridge, who had found himself playing in the reserves earlier in the season in a dispute over pay.

TUESDAY 19TH DECEMBER 2000

An 82nd minute winner from Clinton Morrison, his 14th goal of the season, dumped Premiership Sunderland out of the League Cup and allowed Division One Palace to book a semi-final date with Liverpool. It was the Eagles' third appearance in the last four of this competition.

FRIDAY 19TH DECEMBER 2003

Iain Dowie was officially appointed the new Crystal Palace manager...

SATURDAY 20TH DECEMBER 2003

...but Kit Symons, the caretaker player-manager, took charge of the team the following day and guided Palace to a 3-0 win over Steve Coppell's Reading at the Madejski Stadium.

THURSDAY 20TH DECEMBER 2001

Palace faced Nottingham Forest in league action on a Thursday night thanks to ITV Digital's £315m deal with the Football League, a tie-up that subsequently collapsed forcing a number of clubs into administration after they had spent promised television money that never materialised.

MONDAY 21ST DECEMBER 1953

Brighton & Hove Albion came to Selhurst Park and lost... but this time it was Wrexham who took the spoils as Palace's ground was needed as a neutral venue for a second replay in the FA Cup second round. Glaziers manager Laurie Scott was present and was so impressed with the Welshmen's inside-forward Tommy Tilston he signed him six weeks later. Tilston made 59 appearances for Palace.

SATURDAY 21ST DECEMBER 1996

Neil Shipperley scored three minutes from time to hand Crystal Palace a 1-0 victory over Charlton Athletic in front of 16,279 at Selhurst Park.

SATURDAY 22ND DECEMBER 1956

The floodlights failed after 55 minutes of play at Highfield Road in the league encounter against Coventry City which led to the abandonment of the game.

MONDAY 22ND DECEMBER 1980

Malcolm Allison tried to land Manchester City goalkeeper Keith MacRae but he turned down the opportunity to move.

TUESDAY 23RD DECEMBER 1980

Brighton & Hove Albion chairman Mike Bamber revealed a projected plan for Palace and their south coast rivals to share a stadium at Gatwick.

TUESDAY 23RD DECEMBER 1998

Palace stepped up their interest in Norwich City's Welsh under-21 international Craig Bellamy. An initial bid of £1m was rejected by Mike Walker, but Ron Noades contacted the Canaries with an improved offer.

WEDNESDAY 24TH DECEMBER 1998

Rumours abounded that Palace were close to bringing Dion Dublin to Selhurst Park from Coventry City for a club record fee of £3m, but the player's wage demands proved the stumbling block.

FRIDAY 24TH DECEMBER 2004

Crystal Palace boss Iain Dowie was anxious for highly-rated winger Wayne Routledge to sign a new deal before the January transfer window opened, as the 19-year-old was out of contract in the summer and had been linked with a £3m move away from Selhurst Park; "He's an individual who is the future of this club and we need to get him tied down," remarked Dowie.

MONDAY 25TH DECEMBER 1916

Due to the First World War, football became organised on a much more local level with the national Football League suspended. This benefitted Southern League clubs such as Crystal Palace, for they would now find themselves playing the bigger London teams that plied their trade in the top tier of English football, even if all clubs found themselves affected by military call-ups. Fixtures were double-paired and Palace drew 2-2 against Southampton on Christmas Day morning in a league fixture in the London Combination, followed with another 2-2 draw down at the Dell on Boxing Day.

SATURDAY 25TH DECEMBER 1920

On their way to becoming champions of the Football League Third Division, Crystal Palace faced a Christmas double header with Brighton & Hove Albion. Away on the south coast on Christmas Day, the Londoners grabbed a 2-0 win.

TUESDAY 25TH DECEMBER 1945

Crystal Palace secured the Third Division (South), South Region title when they beat Bournemouth 4-1 at Selhurst Park on Christmas Day morning. It was the Glaziers' third wartime league championship.

WEDNESDAY 25TH DECEMBER 1957

Crystal Palace played their last-ever Christmas Day fixture, going down 3-0 away to Brentford in the Third Division (South).

SUNDAY 26TH DECEMBER 1920

The Nest was packed with 22,000 fans that came to see round two of back-to-back league games with Brighton. Palace did the double when captain Ted Smith hit the winner in a 3-2 victory.

SATURDAY 26TH DECEMBER 1953

Proving that the fixture computer has never really favoured Palace around Christmas, the Glaziers found their request for a local pairing had fallen on deaf ears at the Football League. Boxing Day saw Palace away at Norwich City, having already beaten the Canaries at Selhurst Park 1-0 the day before. The teams travelled to East Anglia together and shared a belated turkey and plum pudding Christmas dinner. But Palace had clearly eaten too much and lost 2-1 at Carrow Road.

SUNDAY 26TH DECEMBER 1910

The first Boxing Day fixture between Crystal Palace and Brighton & Hove Albion was played down on the south coast. Palace lost 2-0.

THURSDAY 26TH DECEMBER 1935

Jack Blackman scored his second hat-trick of December when he bagged three goals in the 5-1 rout of Swindon Town in the Third Division (South).

WEDNESDAY 26TH DECEMBER 1962

Next to bottom in the Third Division, Crystal Palace faced local rivals Millwall in a crucial, must win South London derby at Selhurst Park. Manager Dick Graham was able to play new signings Cliff Holton and Dickie Dowsett together for the first time, but it was former Lion Peter Burridge who put the Glaziers ahead. Dowsett then made it 2-0 when he scored his first goal for Palace, before Ronnie Allen slotted home a late penalty to ensure bragging rights went to the home team.

FRIDAY 26TH DECEMBER 1980

Tony Sealy bagged a brace against Arsenal at Selhurst Park but the Gunners still left with a point as the game ended 2-2. Sealy only ever made 27 appearances for the Eagles.

SATURDAY 27TH DECEMBER 1969

Having lost away to Tottenham Hotspur the day before, Palace welcomed Chelsea to Selhurst Park in front of a record crowd of 49,498. But it was the visiting fans that went home happy as the Blues beat the Glaziers 5-1.

SATURDAY 27TH DECEMBER 1980

Gerry Francis was made player-coach on the same day as Palace lost 3-2 to Brighton & Hove Albion in front of 27,367 at the Goldstone.

FRIDAY 28TH DECEMBER 2001

Palace manager Trevor Francis declared ahead of the Bradford game: "I am still working to get a squad where our performance will not be affected. I am determined to do this at Palace but we need time."

WEDNESDAY 28TH DECEMBER 2005

Palace beat Derby County 2-0 at Selhurst in the Championship with first-half goals coming from Clinton Morrison and Darren Ward in front of 18,978.

MONDAY 29TH DECEMBER 1997

After missing a 78th-minute penalty in the Premiership encounter against Southampton that would have won Palace the match, Itzhik Zohar was given permission to go back to Israel for New Year. But once home, Zohar turned out for his former club Maccabi Haifa in a friendly against AC Milan which he did not have permission for. Ironically, he missed a penalty in that game also and not much was heard from him thereafter.

SATURDAY 29TH DECEMBER 2007

Neil Warnock returned to his hometown club Sheffield United, one he managed for seven and a half years, for the first time since leaving. In front of the Sky cameras, his current team Crystal Palace carved out a 1-0 win thanks to James Scowcroft's first-half strike.

SATURDAY 30TH DECEMBER 1911

Ted Smith got the first of five hat-tricks he would score for Crystal Palace when he plundered three against West Ham United in the Southern League, Division One. Richard Harker also bagged a hat-trick.

SUNDAY 30TH DECEMBER 1990

Palace beat the current league champions Liverpool 1-0 at Selhurst Park, when Mark Bright tucked the ball past Bruce Grobbelaar following a cross from Ian Wright.

TUESDAY 31ST DECEMBER 1997

Palace's New Year's Day Division One fixture against Stoke was called off due to the frozen Selhurst Park pitch. The early nature of the decision allowed players their first New Year's Eve off for many seasons!

SATURDAY 31ST DECEMBER 2005

Andy Johnson fired home a hotly contested 72nd-minute penalty after Clarke Carlisle tussled with Clinton Morrison to secure a 2-1 win and three points for Crystal Palace at Vicarage Road in the Championship. Defender Darren Ward had opened the scoring for the Eagles in the 18th minute, bundling home his second goal in as many games from close range.